The Cape of Joy

Canadian Cataloguing in Publication Data

MacKinnon, Angus Matheson, 1932-
    The Cape of Joy

ISBN 0-9698337-6-8

1. Bible O.T. Psalms--Devotional use. I.Title

BS1451.M32 1999   242'.5   C99-900114-0

The Cape of Joy

Angus Matheson MacKinnon

THE
CATALONE
PRESS

Cover Picture

Rev. Angus with sailing friend Buddy Allen, making November
trip from Sydney to home base in Robert's Pond, Mira Bay, Cape
Breton.   South Head in background.

Photo by Thomas Dickson.

Published by:
The Catalone Press
PO Box 1878
Sydney, NS
Canada

Printed in Canada by Princess Printing Ltd., Sydney Mines, NS

Contents

For 'Billie' MacVicar, a life-long traveller to Sion

Introduction

I introduce this devotional book on the Psalms, with a story from history, a sea story from the reign of Queen Elizabeth I. Headlands, capes, or promontories of land, are the symbols of disaster to those who sail the seas. Many scores of ships have crossed the oceans of this world, only to come to grief, wrecked on a headland, sometimes very near home.

Likewise peaks, or capes or headlands correspond to specific occasions in time which mark our spiritual voyage. Such experiences are connoted with hard things that have brought us low, or even broken our heart. They brought us to know pain and sadness and sorrow in this life.

In cultivating a devotional life, I have found, like others, that the greatest grief can be turned into joy, exquisite joy, that spills over, with an abundance, even more than one soul can take. Hence we share, and that is of the essence, of Christ's teaching. If we keep our best spiritual blessings and try and hoard them up for our own use, they can go 'bad' like the manna in the desert, for the Hebrews. Thus we offer a shared experience of joy.

Don't be put off by the story, although it is about English pirates. We all live our lives like a story that is written.

'We live our lives as a tale that is told.'

(Psalm 90:9)

"One ship goes east, another west,

By the self same winds that blow.

'Tis the set of the sail, and not the gale,

That determines the way they go.

Like the winds of the sea are the ways of time,

As we voyage along through life,

'Tis the set of the soul that determines the goal,

And not the calm or the strife."

Quoted from The Gospel Standard

The Cape of Joy

All looked well for the young English pirate. He was commissioned by the English government to make an extended voyage of plunder to South America and relieve the huge Spanish galleons of their cargo of stolen Peruvian gold and silver, and bring it all back to England for the royal coffers.

Why! Even the Queen of England gave him a letter of best wishes, and it was understood that if he was successful, she would personally honour him with a knighthood, as a national hero.

Francis Drake was also assured that God was on his side. Was he not given a chaplain, Richard Hakluyt, an ordained clergyman of the new national church, declared, independent in Henry VIII's Unilateral Declaration of Independence!

This was an adventure beyond the wildest dreams of any schoolboy, and especially for this Devonshire boy, who, in spite of having never attended school, carried the reputation and honour of England to new, if somewhat notorious heights of national glory. But then, the criteria were different from our advanced age of refined pseudo-puritanical hypocrisy. Kings and generals personally fought at the front with their armies; admirals stood on the poop deck of their battleships, and sometimes died by sword thrust or musket.

Consider briefly the beginnings of this adventure. Drake and his men, 164 in all, had a great sendoff. He had three little ships under his command, the Pelican, (later renamed the Golden Hind), the Elizabeth, called after his illustrious queen, and the Marigold, along with two smaller pinnaces. They were

1

well fitted out all at the expense of the English government.

The chaplain/journalist, Richard Hakluyt, tells us how the little fleet left Plymouth with the ebb tide, sailed along the coast with the sails well filled to a northerly breeze. Even the winter sun seemed to smile above them as they left England on this momentous voyage that would make new maritime history. But when they called in at Falmouth, a storm brought near disaster to the little fleet. Drake's own ship was dismasted, and the Marigold was driven ashore. It looked as if the voyage of great expectations had come to grief before it scarcely began. But Drake brought his crippled ships back to Plymouth, repaired all, and now after this four week delay left England on the 13th of December, 1577 on his three year circumnavigation that would make history.

Having raided and plundered several Spanish ports on the way, Drake sailed southwards making landfall at the Cape Verde Islands. From there he caught the trade winds westwards across the Atlantic ocean to reach Brazil, some 54 days later.

Richard Hakluyt gives us a live account of all aspects of the voyage. They were becalmed for weeks in the Doldrums; they passed the time fishing from the abundance of the sea. Our minister/journalist tells how dolphins were taken aboard. He describes how flying fish landed on deck, and observed how they could not get airborne to return to their aquatic environment because their wings were dried out by the sun. On reaching Brazil, a great storm arose which scattered their ships. We cannot realise fully what this meant. There was no radio communication, nothing to indicate that ships had not foundered. All ships were damaged to some degree; all were making water and required constant pumping. One of the five ships was missing.

A careful co-ordinated search was made, to no avail. It looked as if it was lost. Then on the eleventh day after the storm, the reduced fleet passed a headland, and lo, to the great joy of all, the missing ship, the Cantor, renamed the Christopher, was spotted. There was a reunion; there was a party, a party of great thanksgiving. Just think of it, 'the lost were found, the dead were alive again.'

An experience like that eclipsed the terrors of the storm. Further, the Englishmen went ashore and killed 'large and mighty deer' and caught 'sea wolves' (seals), and fresh water was taken aboard. They recaulked the planking of their little ships with the tide at low water. All the negatives of the past were blotted out. They were replaced or succeeded by positive things, including 'good temperatures and sweet air'. To mark God's goodness to them, the place was named the **Cape of Joy**.

We are all on a voyage through this world. We can be separated and scattered by adversity. But our theme is, restoration, overcoming, the lost being found, the dead being alive again. That is illustrated when we get our stores in the shopping mall of the Book of Psalms. Here all the wares and warnings, all the prophecies and provisions of the rest of Scriptures, can be reflected in the religious experience of the world voyager to Sion, the celestial city. And is that not what every believer is, a sojourner, a traveller, a voyager, a person who 'is going places'? Then for us, like Francis Drake there is the home-coming, the great celebration, the meeting with our Lord, the King of kings. And then there is the knighthood, where we kneel at his throne and rise to be 'kings and priests unto God.' In the words of the hymn writer:

There's love and life and lasting joy,
Lord Jesus, found in Thee.
(B.E. Church Hymnary)

Psalm 3

Lord how are they increased that trouble me! many are they that rise up against me.

Many there be which say of my soul, There is no help for him in God. Selah.

But thou, O Lord, art a shield for me; my glory, and the lifter up of my head.

I cried unto the Lord with my voice, and he heard me out of his holy hill. Selah.

I laid me down and slept; I awaked; for the Lord sustained me.

I will not be afraid of ten thousands of people, that have set themselves against me round about.

Arise, O Lord, save me, O my God: for thou hast smitten all mine enemies upon the cheekbone; thou hast broken the teeth of the ungodly.

Salvation belongeth unto the Lord: thy blessing is upon thy people. Selah.

Wake-up Time

Come my friends and look at this psalm with me. It is an offering of praise to God, rising in the morning to heaven's throne from a human being who knows all the negative experiences that we associate with the night and with the darkness.

When we offer praise to God, we think automatically of transactions of grace, whereby God has met our spiritual requests with the answer of his resources. Our needs with all the groanings and sorrows that lead us to cast ourselves upon God's mercy in prayer, are now answered by the abundance of his grace.

Then we praise God with the heart and with the voice. We seek the Lord alone bringing our burdens to him. When we get a reply from him - just think of it - God bothering to give a reply to you or me- then the heart that was heavy, now rejoices and joins with the rest of God's people singing his praises in the services of worship in our community.

Many psalms are linked to specific occasions in the life of David. But when you think of it, the specific occasion is not as important as the experience to which it is linked. The great thing is the experience by which the psalm of praise is bequeathed to the church for all ages - yes, may it not be for glory itself. Then its purpose has been realised. Further, is it not true, neither David nor any other follower of the Way graduates into a trouble-free dimension, until they are received into glory.

Thus, I am sure if we were to ask David, what was the occasion of this psalm, he might well answer that it coincided with the awful nightmare experience when he fled from Jerusalem because of the rebellion of his son Absalom. But David would look at us and say, 'My friend, the reality is that this has been a recurring experience throughout my journey of faith in this world. But even as the experience began with fear, darkness and night, so it ended like the day breaking, with God's deliverance for my soul.'

One commentator has written that you will find no situation which corresponds to this psalm, though you search the story of David's life from beginning to end. We would say rather, if we read between the lines, throughout David's life, we believe there were many times and occasions that his life experience corresponded to this psalm and its companion, the evening hymn, Psalm 4. And for you and me, we are called to worship God, singing the Psalms all through our pilgrimage and our journey of faith in our generation.

There is something else. Even when our experience does not appear to correspond to the substance of this psalm at any one time, the use of the psalm has a threefold benefit.

First: It reminds us of God's rescue missions in past experiences of our life, that are known only to us.

Second: It keeps the promises of God warm in our hearts and minds, should the chill winds of adversity begin to blow. So that like having warm winter clothes, we are ready with God's remedy for the days and nights which will surely come to us, of need.

Third: We are to think of worship as corporate. The psalms may well have their most tender association in the private experience of the individual, but they represent the corporate experience of the believing church. Throughout the earth at any one time in history as it unfolds, believers are members of the Body of Christ.

Therefore praise will be something outgoing, reflecting the corporate fellowship of the whole church. Thus you and I share in the tribulations and the triumphs of other people, even when there does not seem to be a correspondence between the Psalms that reflect their experiences and our experience.

This is of great significance when we think of the church, as we shall do later in dwelling upon the Psalms. It was the Scottish divine, Dr John "Rabbi" Duncan, who exhorted the fragmented church in 19th century Scotland to beware of neglecting the **communion of the church at large.**

Co-operative complementation

As we anticipate the third millenium of history, since the first Advent of Christ, co-operative complementation of all believers is a prerequisite to the dynamic renewal of His church - remember the church is Christ's and beware of anyone usurping that claim. For anyone or any one group, call it a denomination or a church, it is a spiritual indulgence to live to oneself and an option that appears to be a contradiction of Scriptural teaching. There is a parallel in the secular world, where parties involved in the European union of nations, find that they will be unable to maintain their own specific currency, in a shared economic union. All are part of the whole.

Truly as the political and economic future demands international agreement and co-operation, so also that spiritual kingdom represented by the believing witnesses of Christ, demands a co-operative complementation of resources. In this respect there can be no coercion. The outward expediency must arise from inward principle. And furthermore, the nature of God's kingdom is co-extensive with the universality of all people that dwell upon the earth, black and white, rich and poor, across the whole spectrum of mankind, and in all the varied conditions of Providence.

Thus all individual experiences should, to a greater or lesser extent, always embrace in prayer, meditation, service, and worship, this consciousness of the trans-historical diversity in unity which makes up the church of Christ in its glorious pilgrimage in following Christ.

Individual faith expends itself in community

If we think of belief, we think primarily of the spiritual exercise of the mind and heart. This is related to disposition and attitude. Yet who can measure this in a person or in the collective of the church! Often this may be very real, yet in some way remain ineffectual in the dynamic renewal of the world, and as a testimony in the community. Thus it is, that despite the glory of the spiritual life, which in a believer's heart has exquisite overtones of joy and blessing, as the heart is full of grace and as the mind is stamped with the imagery of the heavenly through the Word, so that the soul is satisfied with God's abundant mercies - in spite of this, round about the believer, there may be many that hunger and thirst and are not led to Christ. The result is that the harvest of the world remains in the field, and is not reaped and gathered in for the kingdom of heaven.

The fact is that there must be the 'down to earth' reality of outward action. The church is not just a people called out, taken off the train of a lost humanity as it hurtles along the railway to its mortal doom. The church is called to stand out. It is like a city set on a hill; a light that shines and cannot be hid. You and I, if we are called by the name of Christ, are chosen in God's elective will to be his witnesses.

A three-fold mandate

But this action is not just unilateral on our part, personally or as denominations. The mandate to the Christian is to act within the framework of the Body of Christ. Implied in this is (a) **to give** (b) **to organise** (c) to submit **to being organised.** Dr Thomas Chalmers who led the church movement in Scotland, social, educational as well as spiritual to its climax in 1843 on the issue of freedom of the church from state interference, called the people to do two things.

1. *Everyone should give a penny a week to the church.*
2. *The church must organise.*

He repeated this: *Organise, organise, organise.* This was done at all levels, in the local congregations and in the highest consultative levels of church personnel. Apart from the building of Divinity Colleges like New College in Edinburgh, the Free Church through its organisation developed education policies to reach the most distant islands, (Viz. Out-Skerries in Shetland), as well as missions educational, medical and evangelistic abroad, and created Colleges of Education like Moray House in Edinburgh for the training of teachers. All this was done within a period of dynamic organisation, a synthesis of the spiritual inspiration and social responsibility, reflecting the vision of Scotland's ecclesiastical visionaries, John Knox, Andrew Melville, Alexander Henderson. In short the Reformed agenda of permeating Christian leaven into the very texture of the State was implemented. And this was realised through the willing participation by the ordinary people in the context of an organised structure of the church. All the lay educational establishments passed to the secular authorities as a gift of the church after the Scottish Education Act of 1872. Much of what is good in Scotland today, has been bequeathed to the secular state by the devotion and diligence exhibited in the past through the organisation of the church. *Laissez-faire* is more often than not an excuse for indolence - and that leads to national disaster and decay.

The same challenge in a changing world

But the church does not throw up its hands, just because there has been a take-over by the secular state. We are called to follow the same threefold principle, *to give, to organise and be organised.* The dynamic witness of the believing church becomes effectual through the deliberate and conscious organisation of people who are committed to the greatest Cause in the world, the kingdom of Christ. In this way, the church becomes the dynamic factor. It is like a mighty army with banners. To perceive things differently is a false and escapist approach which renders witness ineffectual.

The church like a many coloured carpet

It is in sharing in the experience of the church in its magnitude across history, across all the lines of denomination which have been set up to separate and divide the flock of God's sheep, for one reason or another sometimes justified, sometimes questionably so, that the heart is lifted up from the personal experience of despondency. This does not infer a merging of every entity or group so that it ceases to lay a clear emphasis on **its principle doctrinal position**. The church is similar to a carpet that we may purchase from Iran or Pakistan. The carpet has many different colours and design features. Each feature can be vividly different from others in shape and colour. But they all together comprise the whole carpet, so that there is an overall harmony and unity. No one would dream of merging all the colours and eliminating all the separate distinctive features in order to achieve some soul-less anonymous sameness. No more should any co-ordinated co-operation of the multi-faceted church of Christ cause the church to lose its distinctive features in its separate parts. In this comprehensive identity believers share in the glory of the church in all the promises that make her the Bride of Christ.

The heavenly Jerusalem

This is the mother church, the heavenly Jerusalem, that through the advent and indwelling of the Spirit, takes visible form in the church on earth. This heavenly Jerusalem is free, gloriously free, within the parameters of the imperatives of the Spirit.

> *But Jerusalem which is above is free, which is the mother of us all* (Galatians 4:26)

It is the creation of God's grace at work in the hearts of human beings, who are therefore changed, metamorphosed like limestone into marble, oil into propulsion, or electricity into light. In short when human nature is **converted**, you have latent potential for spiritual power. But even that can be dissipated and wasted without the co-ordinated co-operation which makes an integrated and organised organic church the instrument of God's will and purposes for a redeemed humanity.

We know that this entity, the church, is formed for the glory of God. It is in this, the fruit of the Covenant of God's love spelt out in history, but transcending history- for history stops with the cessation of time in contrast to the church continuing throughout eternity - that each believer is part of the whole and has covenant rights to the *inheritance of the saints in light.* I have nothing apart from Christ. But I have not Christ apart from his church. I was not born in a vacuum. I am debtor to the church for the continuity of revelation, for the fire of trial, for the endurance of tribulation, for the testimony of its witness, so often raised in the centuries of the past, at the cost of being faithful even unto death. Who in any generation can separate their personal faith, their little collective, from the campfires of the church's fellowship on a world scale, or dissociate themselves in self-righteous independence from the believers in the early church who were torn asunder in the amphitheatres of Rome or Ephesus, or those in the 17th century, shot on the Scottish moors, while owning primary allegiance to Christ as King, before any other parochial loyalty of nationalism! Truly, when we reflect on the debt we owe to the past witness of the church, even allowing for its short-comings, we have to conclude with the 17th century poet preacher, John Donne that *no man is an island.*

Each believer has a contributing experience

Does it not follow that all the promises of God are not realised within the experience of one believer! If you have an interchange of experiences, you will find that this is an expression of variety. My experience as a believer is not a microcosm of the whole church. It just cannot be. My life covers only a tiny segment of conscious existence relating to time. It requires multitudes to live out the **whole magnitude of the experience of grace**. It is a bit humbling that my little witness would not be missed except by a few personal friends who know me. When I say that, then I remember that Christ my Saviour would miss my presence. For I rest my hopes in this, that it is by his grace I am saved, and that by his power, his Resurrection power I shall have a place in the eternal concert of praise with the redeemed church in glory. It is in the complementation of the experience of all believers in time who make the journey of faith and forsake not the fellowship of other believers, that we entertain the hope of glory and share the corporate union of the redeemed mulititudes with their Risen Lord.

We can use this psalm to praise God at any time

Therefore, my friend, you are called to join in and sing this psalm; it is a song for the morning. It does not matter whether or not it coincides with a specific experience in your life at this point in time; the psalm represents the totality of the church's experience. Do you see the implication of this?

You and I may join in praising the Lord irrespective of our mood. We may be cast down, or feeling on top of the world. We may be weak or we may be strong. We may be going through deep waters, or we may feel that we are on the mountain top. We may feel desolate or be conscious of the nearness of Christ. But whatever the case may be, we are called to praise the Lord. Remember the apostles praised God while in prison.

Praise is dynamic. It rises to heaven as prayer rises like incense. But praise is greater than prayer, because while prayer suggests need, praise is thanksgiving. It seeks nothing but acceptance from God. And God never turns his back on people who praise him. It is a means of grace just to join in with God's people in a church, in a city or in a country chapel. In the mystery of God's elective will, he will cause us to call upon him also in prayer so that we come to know the spiritual requests that are freely available in Christ for the renewal of our lives.

Praise does not wait until all prayers are answered

Praise follows prayer, answered prayer, but we are not called to wait until all our prayers are answered. We are invited to praise God in anticipation, believing in him, even for His own Name's sake. I recall my mother who lived her life in a deep faith. She was always punctuating her busy daily routine in the manse, with short spells of prayer. One of the lasting memories I have of her is seeing her kneeling at the milking stool in the byre, after she had milked the cows. I can picture her yet after fifty years, in the old glebe byre, in Aultbea, her voice rising and falling as she savoured the promises of God which she took to the throne of grace and used to plead before her advocate within the veil, her Risen Saviour.

She had a list of pleas, some for the needs of the family - eight children had plenty needs - the sick and the bereaved, prayer for blessings upon the young, prayers for a blessing on the services of the sanctuary, prayers for revival of religion and honouring of the Lord's Day. I can hear her voice rising and falling in the musical cadences of the Gaelic, that matchless medium of communicating with heaven, expressing all the delicate nuances of our spiritual being, and the inexhaustible variety of provisions, from the storehouses of heaven. As my mother prayed, her voice would seem suddenly to change at one point. It was as if the door of heaven opened to her. Christ had come into her spiritual consciousness and she was seeing him with the perception of her soul, for her eyes would be gently shut to the sensory world about her. Her prayer was then like a conversation with a loved one, a loved one who had all the attributes that we associate with Christ in all his fulness and riches in glory. Then her voice would take on a kind of closing note. Her face flushed with emotion, evinced a new serenity, and her lips would almost break into a smile. Her spiritual therapy was over, her faith was strengthened, her vision was renewed, her tryst with the lover of her soul, the *altogether lovely one and the chief among ten thousand,* the Saviour of the world, was completed. She would rise with grace filling her consciousness, and the fragrance of heaven pervading her being and make her way to the manse, singing softly a hymn of Rev Robert Murray MacCheyne.

How can I forget her and the memories of her devotions! But the specific reason for recalling her at this time is the fact that she went to glory with many, many prayers unanswered. But to the end, her prayers were full of *praise,* and it seemed that every need was another excuse for calling upon her Lord with her gift of praise. There were many choice believers, men and women who had this developed spiritual power with God. The effect of their witness permeated the community and in many ways was a protective shield from evil. We often think only of the evils that happen and forget the many that did not happen. Therefore we should always praise the Lord.

Make our spiritual needs an excuse for praise

We also are called to praise God when we are conscious of burdens and when we feel in bondage; when we are like David, surrounded with enemies, or when we seem to be in darkness. God cannot help hearing and because it is his special work to rescue, to deliver, to save, for Christ is our Deliverer, eventually all our prayers which are in accord with his sovereign will, will be answered, according to his sovereign will.

Keeping the lamps of the sanctuary full of oil

Even when the church is in a period of apathy with many in spiritual slumber, there are believers who keep the lamps of the sanctuary alight. Through their vigil, praise rises to the throne of Heaven, night and day, wherever on earth the sun rises and sets. Indeed the forgotten monks lighting their candles in the monasteries and chanting their songs of praise, throughout the Dark Ages in Europe, represented the only visible continuity, by which Christ's church nurtured the Christian heritage and passed it on from one generation to another, making us, in the world of the 21st century, the beneficiaries.

The case for perpetual praise

There is a strong case for a perpetual offering of praise being continually offered to God in a community church. This is not new. The Moravians pursued this practice. From it came the radical religious revival in the Church of England, a revival that the class structure with its historic rigidity and reactionary views could not accept. Hence the English Disruption known as Methodism. How often we are strangers to the sanctuary except at set times of services, which may well be only for an hour a week on the Lord's Day. The location could vary. It could be sometimes in the sanctuary, sometimes in a hall or even in a house in the community, especially where there was a shut-in or an invalid. One could envisage that relays of groups of two or three could in turn carry on this ministry. Use could also be made of the technological advantages we enjoy to keep the praise of God continually being heard. Would this not bring the promise of hitherto unknown but glorious expectations to people, individually and to the congregation in its worship! Think of the fruits of that kind of local organisation.

(a) There would be an open church so that anyone could come and join in worship.

(b) There would be a greater acquaintance with the Psalms, for they are certainly without equal, the manual for that continuous praise along with the great hymns of the church.

(c) All the needs of people could be brought before the Lord, in the context of the church, and presented as supplication to God.

(d) And think of it; you would not have a spasmodic light of worship shining for an hour once or twice a week. Rather, there would be a continuous song, so that praise of God, which is linked to dynamic spiritual power would be a force to reckon with, in the context of a world where evil is certainly no stranger.

(e) The congregation would be exercising its spirituality, which is surely the very reason for its existence. It is right that Christians should assert their spiritual contribution as a social unit over against other community clubs and associations that have a specific rather than a general appeal.

We should ask ourselves in the church, Why should there be continuous relays of songs of the world on radio and by other means, while praise to God our Creator and Redeemer should last but a few minutes during one or two services a week? This simple expedient would give individuals to feel that they were all wanted, that their voice counted, that the continuity of the collective intercessory praise at the gates of heaven, would so characterise the congregation, that God himself would both hear and answer in a visitation of his Spirit with all the glorious blessings that would accompany this. I believe that this is perfectly feasible, if we in the church were organised in a pragmatic systematic external manner in every community.

This is not to suggest that Christians are not praying in the secret place for God's blessing and praising Him. But in the organised relay of continuous praise in the public venue or selective home or hall, there would be the seed sown for spiritual expectations to be fulfilled. Then the world would see that the church was no longer sleeping, but was marshalled in divisions, in regiments, in brigades, in battalions and in humble companies and platoons. Yes, it would be seen like an army with banners, ready with all the weapons of the Spirit, to do battle in the name of Christ, and bring victory to many lives in every community, the victory of faith in overcoming, and the triumph of joy in believing.

Organisation could justifiably be designated a means of grace. It is not to be despised as a pragmatic non-spiritual deployment of our energies - a kind of secondary requirement for second rate Christians. Of course organisation is essentially an expedient, a means to an end. Well, is not the service in the sanctuary also an expedient and rightly called *the means of grace*? It may in some respects be as necessary for the church as the shell is to the egg, or the skilled shepherding is to the welfare of the sheep. What a transcendent testimony could follow from sanctified organisation. And what wonderful joy would come from such corporate witness and participation. Also people are justifiably sceptical about the ecclesiastical boundaries as valid in the world of today.

Time for a new strategy

It may well be that that species of organisation along doctrinal lines of emphasis, is simply not sufficient to meet the requirements for Christ's strategy for world conquest. We tend to think of the church as the ecclesiastical, as if the two are synonymous. Strictly speaking the church could scrap the present visible organisation visible to the world, in the buildings, church holdings in the Stock Market, its huge land and city holdings, for instance held by the Anglicans in England and the Presbyterians in Scotland. It makes sense. It might be a good thing if there was another Thomas Cromwell - do not confuse him with Oliver Cromwell - on the scene who would repeat Henry VIII's acquisition of the Church's wealth. The Roman Catholic Church indeed grew rich. But let it be remembered that Ewart Gladstone, the British 19th century prime minister, saw the Protestant Episcopal Church in Ireland just as culpable, and sequestered half of the riches of the Church to be given to the state. There might be a howl from the prelates and the church managers and trustees, but it might be a real opportunity for the church to rediscover itself and find a new form of organisation as an expedient to serve the spiritual purposes for which the church exists. The ecclesiastical patterns are visible expedients for the building of the spiritual.

We learn from, though not necessarily emulate skills from the secular world. Spiritual wisdom does not infer inefficiency. The church is prone enough to follow precedents of the world when it suits its own perceived purposes. If fulfilling the purpose of God is the primary motivation there should be no hesitation in adopting expedients which are proven in secular spheres like industry. For example, in 1994 computer manufacturers in the United States found that the time tested expedient of production of the Assembly line, introduced by Henry Ford in making his famous Model T automobile in the 1920's and adopted in industry as infallibly the best method of production since then, is no longer suited to the new age of technology. It has proved to be unnatural for workers, and because of sickness and dullness, induced in its inherent monotony and repetitiveness, the result is inefficiency.

In the previous decade, industry had become aware of this and various experiments were tried, some utilising robots. Enough to say that in 1994, one computer company COMPAC which had been on the economic slide, adopted group production. In contrast to the assembly- line method where a person did one production action repetitively, by the group method, two, three, four, five or six workers produce a production unit, for instance the computer, from beginning to testing and final packing. Within months the expedient showed itself to be a key factor not only in efficient production costs, but also in the increased well-being, work related *morale* of the workers, not to mention the increase in their earnings.

In the sphere of the spiritual, ecclesiastical organisation should be viewed in the same light. Take away the sentiment, take away the layers of sterile tradition, peel off the old paint coats of glorified prejudice, of provincial bias, of secular compromise, of intermarriage with superstition-based puerile groups, not to mention national and political liaisons, then we can see the church for what it really is, a spiritual structure of dynamic liaison between God and people living a life of order and joy through the redeeming love of Christ

The denominational divisions have had a good innings and have scored many victories for God's work of the spirit. But the church should examine new strategies of organisation. The spiritual comprises the essence of the church. But the essence is not the ecclesiastical structure or pattern. St Paul presents in his letter to the Ephesians the concept of the church as a spiritual structure. John A. MacKay, Principal of Princeton ,in his Croall Lectures in Edinburgh just prior to the formation of the World Council of Churches in Amsterdam in the 1950's, explores St Paul's perceptions and gives the Letter to the Ephesians the title of 'God's Order.' He speaks of the church not as a dream or ideal to be wistfully longed for and projected in the beautiful imagery of the poets, and the contemplations of the mystic monks. Nor was it the conceptual and composite edifice based upon the reasoned analysis of nature and the result of wisdom's discovery of truth and absolutes in natural revelation. For St Paul the structure of the church was already there. But there was scarcely any visible ecclesiastical pattern. Therefore the structure was identified as the essence. The essence was there, the executive of God's will, to claim the earth and its peoples for Christ.

That brings us to look for the essence and the structure wherever believers form cells of community faith, big or small. It reverses our thinking. Instead of looking at such fellowships and justifying them as the true church by their correspondence with the ecclesiastical union, we look at the ecclesiastical union, council denomination or whatever, and validate it, as it corresponds to the same criteria to which the local cell or community of faith is accredited.

There is no doubt that for St Paul, any claim to be in the church of Christ must be tested in terms of inclusive identity with the whole spectrum and diversity of believers. The penitent prostitute who anointed the Saviour with the precious ointment must be accepted along with the devout prelate who uses his position in the ecclesiastical system as an expedient for spreading the love of Christ and affirming the royal law of the Saviour. This puts the onus for accreditation right back to the cell of community faith. No one lives to himself, and no Christian cell of believers is independent from the organic Body of Christ.

The second essential criterion is discipline, variously interpreted and more variously applied but unquestionably embracing acceptance of God's holiness and the mandatory obedience of the Moral law.

The third criterion must be the proof of spiritual life. That exhibits itself in an effusion of love to one another within the fellowship and outward to others, in active witness, to the Victory of Christ on Calvary.

The church is nothing without being spiritual

Surely this leads us to think of the *spiritual* as primary in contrast to orthodoxy and credal subscription as the key to church life! It means that within the Pauline and Scriptural parameters, the church can start all over the place like a person who takes a torch from a bonfire and starts new little fires round about. Just think of it, *where two or three are gathered together* in Christ's name- that is the church, not just in embryo, but in fulness. These few believers in a church on the prairie or in a basement prayer group meeting on a university campus in Paris can experience all the fulness of blessing of God's presence.

The strength, then, of this new *organised praise* that might be at least considered, is in this, namely that its genesis is in the local community. The co-operation required would enlist all congregations who believed in co-operative complementation. Again, no one could start any critical bickering if the psalms were used as the manual of praise along with the agreed immortal hymns like Amazing Grace and Abide with Me, which with others are already in the *top-ten.*

The effect on individuals could well be the prelude to transforming experiences of grace. It is not extravagant to conceive of large-scale revival and renewal of the church, even to the overflowing of that grace beyond the seeming insularity of the church, into the surrounding community.

The powers of darkness cringe before the manifestation of God's power. No door can remain closed when the latent forces of heaven reflected in God's praise on the lips of people, *enter the ring*, in the fight for righteousness.

The world waits for the church to make a move

In the third millenium the world waits for the church to make a move. Of course the power is of God; the ecclesiastical collaboration of compromise and polite omission of distinctive beliefs are on the other hand, spiritually sterile, and invite the death wish upon the church. But we are not to back into a corner of negative siege; we are to go forward with the diligence of faith, and the wisdom of righteousness. In the dedicated commitment of regular and communal worship perpetually rising to heaven as lighted candles before the throne of God, we set the stage for the life -giving visitation of God's Presence through his Holy Spirit. When the Holy Spirit comes upon a people, few or many, then glorious things are sure to happen, like the bursting forth into blossom of trees after a long winter of darkness. Many who were of the world yesterday, are now counted willingly as the people who are **born of the spirit** and whose hope is in **Christ their Redeemer**. Hear that, - grace does wonders and those who join to praise the Lord in the perpetual presentation of worship, are bound to represent a great variety of testimony to what God has done for their souls.

This psalm reflects varied needs

This psalm before us is a morning offering for all who found a solution to life's deepest needs, in God's perfect peace. The experience of the Body of believers is as divergent as the night and the day. Joys so fill the heart that the experience at times is like a day without any shadows, when Christ shines like the sun and the soul bathes, yes, sunbathes in his spiritual light and revels in the warmth of the sun of righteousness.

At other times, sorrows so fill the heart, that the experience is like the night, so dark that there is no relief and the soul longs and waits for the morning with anguish and such heaviness that the silent darkness reflects spiritual desolation and a feeling of being utterly forsaken.

The spiritual dependence syndrome

You know how a pet dog misses its absent master or mistress. You lock the house door and tell the dog not to worry or be anxious and that you will be back soon. You point to the food and the dish of water. But these are little comfort to the dog. His master is away and he is forlorn. There is no substitute for his presence. He will not find peace until his master returns. You see even the dog cannot live by bread alone. It has to have affection. It lives on love. That distinguishes it from being an animal of the wilds. It has come to know the fellowship of you or me, the owner, and for better or for worse, its life is bound up primarily, not with food but with fellowship of its owner and friends. It is part of human society and it rejoices in the fellowship of its master.

How much more do we as human beings who have come to know the ineffable love of Christ, depend for our happiness upon the presence of our Master! Believers feed on this, they drink of this. Without the sense of the presence of Christ by the Holy Spirit abiding with them, they are desolate. It is wonderful for us, that though Christ is not present with us, He is with us in spirit, and we can rejoice in that positive experience of believing. O how the soul can rejoice in the Lord! But O how the soul can yearn and weep without the Lord! Remember, neither experience is unique to any one person, nor is it the monopoly of any individual.

But it is true that we can look at a particular case or experience of a believer and as we reflect upon it, we become aware of the whole experience of the church. By this our understanding of it is increased and we are better prepared when our own experience coincides with that of the church.

David's experience

Psalm 3 represents such a case. It is a glorious testimony to what God has done - for praise is a reflection of what is of God and his grace; prayer reflects what is of man and his needs. Look briefly at David's situation, taking the ruptured relations with his son Absalom as one occasion for the possible composing of this psalm. David had fled from Jerusalem and makes his way into the desert. The decision to leave before Absalom would attack Jerusalem was one of urgent haste, so that there was little or no time for preparation and none to reflect upon it. Thus David finds himself in the desert country in Hebron - what thoughts must have come to him as he spent the nights again under the stars, as he had done so many years before, in his guerrilla struggle for the throne against the house of Saul! Here we find him lying down after a long day. There was much to think upon, all the calamitous events of his son's rebellion, the alienation of many of the people, his abandonment by longtime friends, not to mention the heartbreaking tragic break-up of his family. All this suddenly came before his mind as he lay down to rest. Remember he was no longer young and vigorous, but 'up in years'.

It appeared that the vision of the aspiring young hero, the shepherd poet, the boy who was well-favoured by God and man, had come to nothing. Darkness covered all and in place of Divine favour and popular affection, David was a cast-off, a has-been, discarded on the dunghill of history. It all came home upon him, and because he was a sensitive, poetic, awakened soul, whose spiritual consciousness related to love, his heart bled, and his soul was laden with heaviness.

It was natural for David to review the different factors which had contributed to this experience of desolation. Thus his mind brought different pictures before his soul, just like a video film which we might look at, in our home, after being away on holiday.

As he lay down, David realised that the numbers of people who chose to follow Absalom, were increasing. **Lord how are they increased that trouble me and many are they that rise up against me.**

From what he had been told all the tribes of Israel had sided with the rebellion, and only little Judah was left on the side of the king. But history teaches that you cannot go by numbers - remember Gideon (read Bk of Judges 7:7). Numbers are not the key to success or failure. Now we come to an interesting psychological factor.

David reflected upon what people were thinking about his faith. **Many there be which say of my soul, There is no help for him in God.**

Altogether, by any standard it was a grim picture. The once popular king, who was acclaimed by tens of thousands, was written off, and more than that, many believed that God had written him off as well. Now, this is a very important point. People are so fickle, so shallow in their friendship, that as a rule, when we think of popularity, crowds follow a candidate for leadership in almost any field and give him their vote, only as long as there is the presumption that he is well-favoured. The contrast is seen in the so-called born-winner as opposed to the born-loser. If people believe that you are a winner, you will have crowds round you. If they think you are a loser, off they go to support someone else.

But this is where the **perspective of faith** contradicts that supposedly sacred cow of inexorable logic. Certainly the film of reflection on the factual situation that filled David's mind with negative thinking and brought his spirits to a low ebb, was inaccurate.

(a) His imagination led him to think that more people forsook him than actually did so. Beware of imagination. Never give the reins of your thinking over to your imagination. Of course it can be used to visualise glorious things and lead to creative wonders. But it can more easily visualise falsehood and therefore be very misleading.

(b) The quality of those who remained faithful to David, comprised the elite of the advisers of the kingdom. Numbers are always suspect and large numbers can evaporate quickly. Was not this proven in the victory of Robert Bruce with his little army over the forces of the English, ten times larger, at the battle of Bannockburn in 1314!

(c) God had already chosen David and his work was not yet finished. He was like Daniel, the beloved of the Lord, God's chosen vessel to be filled with the needed grace to do God's will on earth. What more could any young man or woman want in this world, than the conviction that he or she was God's beloved, and God's chosen one to be used in a calling to serve Him and humanity in his or her generation! Now there could be no presumption on the part of David, as there can be none on the part of any other believer, however well favoured he or she may be. God is sovereign. He can give or withhold. But God is never untrue to his promises. He never lets any believer down. God's promises can be relied upon, like a rope we may use to tie an anchor which we trust, will not give way. He is never so occupied with some other case, or distracted by other burdens, that he will not be able to help, when one, yes, one, of his own chosen people is in distress.

But that leads to the key factor, **What did David do in his trouble,** as he reviewed in his mind the grim picture of the events that had overtaken him?

He cried to God

The psalm is addressed to God. It opens with this beautiful devotional word of greeting, **Adonai,** (My Lord) There is a sacred softness in the tone, an absence of presumption, an intrinsic authentic spirituality about it that reminds us that this cry was from a seasoned soldier, a long-time traveller on the road to Sion, and a man who had followed the Lord from his youth. But more, it accords also with the view of David as being very human, and as history has testified even by his own admission, that he had fallen into sin, specific sins, time and again, and exhibited the proneness to go astray, which like a mischief-maker stalks the believer in every age and keeps him dependent upon God's grace. But if this is so, we can also visualise his cry reaching the throne of heaven. It is like an S.O.S. There in the sorting room of prayers, from across the continents of the earth, there is this prayer, this urgent prayer. And it is prefaced by this, **Adonai,** My Lord and my God.

Who is it from? The answer is, It is from David. He is in straits. He has taken every step in political and military skill, but he is at his wits end. He is really low. His imagination is getting the better of him. He cannot sleep. The thoughts of all the negative happenings and to crown it all, the break-up of his family, mean that he is very broken.

And can you not visualise the God whom David trusted and who loved David, turning now to this boy poet shepherd king, to answer as only God can do for David and every one of us. Listen to David as he gives us this morning song, and recounts to us the elements which changed the agitation and despair of darkness into the peace and hope of a new day.

The cure for insomnia

Remember the grim circumstances, the shattering of family ties, the break-up of the kingdom, Against this background of unrelieved gloom, David testifies,

I laid me down and slept: I awaked; for the Lord sustained me.

You see the sequence The night began with the grim review of his situation. He was filled with anxiety. Do we not all identify with him? If we do not take our worries to bed with us, they follow us up the stairs, hop into bed with us and next thing we embrace them and they tangle us up so that we become their prisoner. Can you not see it, just like a large octopus encircling us in its tentacles, so that we are in straits! But my friend if you can relate to this, and who does not, if we are honest with ourselves, let it be also true that we follow what David did. He cried then to God. He fell asleep. He woke up refreshed. He put it all together into this morning song for the church to use through the ages to come, and believers individually to use as a cure for insomnia.

This verbal cure is like a formula which evolved from proven experience. It is given to the church in this personal testimony. We can think of David calling to God. They knew each other. And you and I need only put ourselves in the place of David, and God will also hear our prayers too. But more, we know that this prayer was answered, because David tells us the result. He slept soundly. Why? I thought he was agitated and distressed and at his wits' end? Yes, but God answered his prayer and David says, that he slept soundly, because **God sustained him.** The Hebrew word literally means, **support.** That's it; God supported him. He had been falling apart spiritually. But God was not delayed by light years of distance. He was there on the spot, just as he is for every one of us to enjoy when we are full of blessing, and to be our support system when we are like David, the victim of anxiety and therefore of insomnia. We have to take God at his word. You cannot rely on two supports at one time, if they are opposite in nature, or diametrically opposed. So that we as human beings cannot rely upon worldly support systems which conflict with spiritual good. The worldly support systems may even be spiritual yet be essentially opposed to the spiritual strength that comes from God in Christ, that makes the weak strong, and calms the anxious spirit.

David could not fall apart now, because the everlasting arms of his Maker and Redeemer were upholding him. This is the therapy for anxiety and insomnia. Casting all our care upon him, our heavenly Father, crying out with our voice to him, to come and help us. Of course there are situations which cause us to be agitated and keep sleep from our eyes. God does not drug us as we use sedatives to deaden our consciousness. This has a place and a very essential one, by which we are alert to possible danger and calamity for our own and the life of others. But when we are agitated and at the end of our resources, and seemingly outnumbered and overwhelmed by events and circumstances, He shows us, even as we call upon him, that He is our Redeemer, a redeemer that is mighty. He is one who never puts to shame any who lean upon him.

David does not relate all the intimate details of the transactions of grace which went on between him and God that dark night. There is no tape recording; there is no video of God's visitation; there are no pictures of the everlasting arms lifting David; there is no contrast recorded of the agitated face raised to heaven, and then the serenity of that face as David slept literally in the arms of his Saviour. No, we are not told of any long prayer, how long David cried before God visited him with an answer.

I do not believe that there was any such spiritual exercise that night. We do know there were other times when David indeed was kept waiting, as he relates in Psalm 40. But here we are not told that it was like that at all. Rather, God read the situation, and in an instant touched one of his beloved disciples. The effect was a miracle. But then what do you expect when God, the Creator God the Redeemer, God the Sustainer with all his power, touched a needy human being? David relaxed in perfect rest.

How could he, you ask, with all the real troubles he had to face? Well, that is part of the miracle of God 'touching us' with his power. Our extremity is God's opportunity. David relaxed in perfect rest, not because he had his misfortunes reversed. God does not as a rule do that. Calamities happen to the just and to the unjust. But David relaxed in perfect rest because he knew God, his God heard him; because he was sure God loved him; and because he was convinced that God was in charge. In short as he put it, he relaxed and anxiety left him, **because the Lord sustained him.**

Is that not the explicit uncomplicated message that we have in this song, when David awoke to a new day, reflected on the course of events and the night that was over and testified,

> **I laid me down and slept; I awaked for the**
> **Lord sustained me.**

This is offered to us as God's therapy for sleeplessness and all the anxieties that prevent us from a healthy rest. We are told that in this age of increased leisure, in North America, sleeplessness is one of the chief maladies affecting people. Because of this, there is a boom in the drug trade, and psychiatrists and physicians and every variety of spiritual crank are making hay while the sun shines- in an attempt to cure this increasing feature of a superficial society.

And all the time, the Lord of heaven is waiting with the therapy of his grace and the efficacy of his atoning peace for the health of our minds, our souls, our hearts and our bodies.

We quote from another choice psalm,

In dwellings of the righteous
is heard the melody
***Of joy and health:** the Lord's right hand*
doth ever valiantly
(Psalm 118:15)

This is God's therapy for sleeplessness. He deals with the underlying causes, through his redeeming grace, even as we believe in the efficacy of Christ's Finished Work on the Cross of Calvary. Through his saving work on our behalf, we have peace with God, and therefore even in the midst of trouble, we are warranted to relax, though there is a tumult round about us. This redemptive work of Christ is our support system and it will keep the believer buoyant in the deepest waters..

This personal testimony of David is used in another song of praise as a prescription, - that's right ,a prescription - for all who have group insurance as members of the Body of Christ, his church. We see it in Psalm 127

It is vain for you to rise early or sit up late, to
*eat the bread of sorrow: for so **he giveth his***
beloved sleep.

What glorious privileges those who are disciples of the Lord have on earth here as well as the unspeakable joys of eternity! No wonder we are encouraged in our devotions to take the prayer of the Psalmist and dovetail it into our praise as we sing together in worship in the sanctuary.

Remember me Lord with that love
which thou to thine dost bear
With thy salvation, O my God,
to visit me draw near.

That I thy chosen's good may see,
and in their joy rejoice;
And may with thy inheritance
triumph with cheerful voice.

(Psalm 106:4 - 5)

Then, believingly we will say each night as the shadows lengthen, even as the cares and burdens of life threaten to overwhelm us.

I will both lay me down in peace and sleep:
for thou Lord only makest me to dwell in safety.

(Psalm 4:8)

You see, we do not even need to let our troubles get us down. Before we let worry get a grip of us and tear us to pieces, we can call upon God straight away to pre-empt our agitation. Just try this and if you are at present caught suddenly and overwrought, you are never too late for God's emergency service laid on day and night round the clock. And when you have proved it for yourself, you will have this testimony which of course you will share with other needy people,

I laid me down and slept;
I awaked; for the Lord sustained me.

This is a song for the morning. This is a song of peace and joy of refreshing and vitality. Each day you rise, this can be yours, a morning when the sun rises, a morning without clouds a morning with hope and praise for another day.

The assertion of a new confidence

When David went to bed the previous night, he was visited with very alarming fears. Listen to him now, as he sings this morning song.

I will not be afraid of ten thousands of
people, that have set themselves against me
round

Here is undoubtedly a new confidence which is born of God and his ineffable love. David has confided in God and now you have the picture of a renewed man.

I think I see the man of long ago, the young man, believing in Jehovah, going out to battle against the giant of the Philistines, armed only with a shepherd's sling. Something of that pristine faith of youth is back again in the David who rose up this morning, so many years later. Do you see the very exercise of seeking the Lord and resting upon him, has the effect of renewal, of restoring a person! That was true for David and the same sequence works for you and me, making us feel the confidence of being young and strong. Scripture is strewn with assertions of this therapy, like the daisies that keep coming up on the new mown grass. It is a spiritual confidence that contradicts the ageing process and confounds the pundits who calculate that we are finished, written off by God and man as a failure.

> *He giveth power to the faint; and to them that have no might he increaseth strength.*
> *Even the youths shall faint and be weary, and the young men shall utterly fall:*
> *But they that wait on the Lord shall renew their strength; they shall mount up with wings as eagles; they shall run and not be weary; and they shall walk, and not faint.*

(Isaiah 40:29-31)

Listen to Isaiah again in the next chapter reassuring his people Israel. And that includes the Christian church in all ages and those in it who are intimidated by the apparent size and sound of the popular antagonists of the Christian faith.

> *Behold all they that are incensed against thee shall be ashamed and confounded: they shall be as nothing; and they that strive with thee shall perish.*

Thou shalt seek them, and shall not find them,
even them that contended with thee: they that
war against thee shall be as nothing, and as a
thing of nought.

For I the Lord will hold thy right hand, saying
unto thee, Fear not; I will help thee.
Fear not, thou worm Jacob, and ye men of
Israel; I will help thee, saith the Lord, and thy
redeemer, the Holy One of Israel.

(Isaiah 41:11-14)

You see how David had a new confidence! And this was not unique to David. The Lord loved David, but he loves us too (He loves the world) and is waiting at the door of our hearts with baskets of blessings and wants us to connect up to the source of spiritual power that flows from Christ and the power of his Resurrection, to give people a new confidence, based upon the infinite resources of God that we use by exercising faith. We can then do all things through Christ who strengtheneth us. We can run any number of appliances in every department of human activity - all in implementing our Master's will, in redeeming society and rescuing people so that they share in the glory that God has prepared for them that love him.

Hear this confidence put another way, as a new consciousness of strength in confrontation against opposition. Here it is in the verse of the Scottish Psalter. I invite you to join in, repeating aloud, this verse. Power, spiritual power will accompany the words as you sing them. Keep doing this. And the effect upon you will fill you with wonder.

Against me though an host encamp
My heart yet fearless is
Though war against me rise
I will be confident in this.

(Psalm 27:3)

34

That confidence is never separated from faith. Faith rests in God and it generates not only power but continual desires for God. Faith multiplies desires in the heart. And the soul develops an insatiable desire for Christ. Yes, the soul craves for God and finds food and delight in seeing Him, as the Spirit accompanies the Word, in revealing the beauty of Christ in all his loveliness to the human soul. Thus in that comparative Psalm of confidence, the Psalmist goes on to say,

> *That I the beauty of the Lord*
> *Behold may and admire*
> *And that I in His Holy Place*
> *May reverently enquire.*
>
> (Psalm 27:4)

This assertion of confidence is almost a challenge to opposition, in whatever guise it appears, against a society governed by Christ and his law. This is a militant anti-force against evil. It is not passive. Remember here is a testimony. God gives his witnesses a testimony so that others will hear and know that people exercise faith in communion with the living God. It does not matter how weak they were, how run-down, how spent; it does not matter if they were discarded on the scrap heap of life, like old electric batteries; it does not matter though they were by-passed as has-beens and dismissed by their peers, they are now connected up to the spiritual power source of heaven. Like David they make a come-back. And there is a challenge in this. Who will stand against them? Who will condemn them? Let anyone try. We are called in the church to go on the offensive, to make a counter-attack. Read the sequel in David's story. (2 Samuel 17,18)

We have this put in a matchless and universal way, as truly a concept inherent in a practical and personal faith in Christ.

> *The Lord stood with me*
> *And strengthened me.*
>
> (2 Timothy 4:17)

That was a confrontation with evil in the context of the church life. St Paul says, Look, this a general principle which I have proved and you and all believers can prove it too. *I can do all things through Christ which strengtheneth me.* And in the NEB we have,

> *I have the strength to face all conditions by the*
> *power that Christ gives me.*

(Philippians 4:13)

When God's power is thus operative in us through Christ, we do not just have the boosting of auto-suggestion, though that is not without its merits. There is now a new or renewed confidence of faith, by which David, or you and I are both humble and at the same time strong. There is a new sense of well-being; a sense of being a winner, *strong in the Lord and the power of his might.* Get this confidence and a person becomes a **new man or woman.**

The ascription of all power and good to God

What a way to begin the day, giving all praise and glory to God! You feel good; you have had a wonderful sleep; and this leads straight away to thinking of God, and your thoughts of God are thus, that He is responsible for all the positive pervasive feelings that make you confident. **The Lord has sustained me.**

Do you see, by ascribing the praise to God, as the source of strength, you are giving your testimony; you are witnessing. It came from the conviction of personal experience. You recognise that you do not have a monopoly of this. You cannot corner the market of grace. You just do not want to. There is an impelling force, which drives you to get others to come to this source of strength as well. You are in effect saying to others, "Come with me to the Lord and seek him; come with your cares and your concerns, your agitation and your anguish. Prove it. God has answered me and given a glorious peace through his covenant of redeeming love." That's it. When you wake in the morning, seek him early and give thanks, for he is not only the source of power that calmed your fears in the dark watches of the night, but he is also the continuing source of power throughout the day before you. He is mighty; he never fails. And through a big faith, you can continue to know his power..

> *For the Kingdom of God is not a matter of words*
> *but of power*

(Ist Corinthians 4:20) NEB

Therefore your life now will be infused with a new range of abilities, a hitherto untapped source of spiritual strength that makes you able to do all things through Christ who strengthens you. **Now you are strengthened with might in the inner man** (Ephesians 3:16), through the continual exercise of faith. You see the point. Is not faith more than worthwhile! You have the secret of power. *The secret of the Lord is with them that fear him.* Why should you lose a day of this new power? Why should anyone let a day go by without exercising faith and ascribing all power to God and all good that we are called in Christ to enjoy?

This Christian life-style is new

This now becomes a life style. You have now joined a universal life style. It does not belong to a day, a passing fashion, a popular change, a generation craze. No, this life style joins you to the Ancients, to those like Enoch who **walked** with God, who like Abraham **talked** with God, who like Jacob **wrestled** with God and **prevailed** and had power with him. All through the centuries there is a continuous procession who lived, and live and shall live, in the realm of time and whose destiny is in the ultimate transformation of their lives when they are clothed with immortality. There is no sitting down and musing over all this however wonderful this may be. This life style is dynamic, for people on the move, the 'get-things-done people' who change the world. And unworthy though you may be like me, you become a transmitter of Good News, of God's redeeming love. And this can reach out to those who might be on the edge of despair. We say this, even as we reflect with anguish on situations where we failed, where we felt there was an unbridgeable gap between us and even loved ones - and we lost them. How humbling to face this, that whatever gifts of grace we may be given by God, we are not autonomous. We would be overcome with anguish because of our failures, but we lay these before our Lord and find relief and peace in believing that beyond the veil of our knowledge, loss, failure even death will through Christ, be converted to victory.

We can do only our part. We can reach out, we can declare, we can tell, but ultimately, in the nature of things, we look for a response; we look for an open hand; we listen for a voice saying, Yes, I will; we look for a face turning round; we wait for a return, or a gesture of desire. There is a sadness that accompanies the human delegated stewardship of our life, whereby even God does not appear to cross the bridge of our will. So that the will is like a security guard standing inside the door of our heart. How glorious when the will responds and lets the power of the Saviour in, with all the implications to give us to be healed, forgiven, restored, renovated like an old house so that we become new. And to crown it all to make us the children of God, through adoption - read Paul's letter to the Romans, chapter 8 and 9 - whereby we also adopt a new life style, the life style of the people of God, who have life more abundant.

Facing the humbling of our own limitations

Where others are passive in this respect, or where we are unable to elicit a response, we are in the area of faith and prayer. The outcome may be apparent tragedy, the loss of a potentially fruitful life, the waste of opportunity of service, the denial of responsible stewardship, the neglect of the means to be transformed. But we have to leave all to God. What else can we do? We are not autonomous and while faith introduces us to glorious certainties for ourselves, it also must include the limitless redemptive power of the same God and redeemer for others, in his sovereign will.

God does not ask a whole lot of theological questions when we call upon him with a broken heart. He does not grill the enquirer to see if he has orthodox views of theology. God's great work is to bind up. He anoints, he touches with his healing power. He calms the agitated spirit. Yes, he literally soothes the furrowed brow and gives us the therapy of sleep. What a peace, what a rest, relaxing in the arms of a loving Saviour.

Of course, rise early, shake off sleep and straight away send a call to heaven of thanksgiving, of adoration. Join with the Body of Christ and sing this anthem of praise.

> **The Lord sustained me. Salvation belongeth unto the Lord; thy blessing is upon thy people**

But we cannot leave this morning song of praise which David bequeathed to the church, without putting these points before you.

The life-style of the believer is full of contrasts

Our lives are full of contrasts, between joys and sorrows, work and leisure, hope and despair, expectation and despondency. The great thing about this Psalm is that it introduces us to a life style where we cease to be at the mercy of circumstances or even of changeable inward personal moods.

It is as if you are now like a ship that has been given ballast. Without the ballast a ship bounces all over the sea, making many people sea-sick. Put the right amount of ballast deep down in the hold or the bilges - I stress this, the right amount of ballast, no more no less - and the ship stays on an even keel, the propeller ceases to rise out of the sea with shuddering vibration. Now the ship surges forward with even power, rising and falling gently, as it proceeds on its voyage.

A believer just cannot get bored

That is a picture of the contrast which so often obtains between those who are strangers to God, and on the other hand those who are strong in the Lord and the power of his might. This does not mean monotony. There will be healthy contrasts filling life - in this new life-style, with variety and excitement. You can spend yourself, give yourself out completely in love and compassion every day. The Lord knows there are enough aching hearts and desolate souls that need the ministry of love. You will go to bed exhausted, but somehow full of a great joy so that as your thoughts rise to dwell upon the Saviour who loves you and the Master whom you serve, sleep will come to you like wine. And the contrast is that, using David's formula, you will wake again in the morning refreshed and ready to face the challenges of another day.

Proving God's Word

You now have limitless credit at the bank of faith. Mention His own Word, quote from its promises. Speak of the unsearchable riches of Christ. I guarantee, yes, I stake my very life upon it, that you will receive more abundantly than you can ask or even think, to meet the demands of living this new life-style of grace and doing the will of God.

We are in continual contact with our God

Once we have experienced the therapy of heaven, like David long ago, we will get to know the Lord. You see what happens. Our trials and anxieties can really be the means of something better. They were the occasion for us to cry unto the Lord. Then the Lord's strength in turn was the means of our salvation, our deliverance, our new life of faith, our new capability to cope with any situation.

Now we love the Lord because of his great love to us. Now we know what God is like. We fear the Lord with a holy fear, that is we reverence him, we give glory to him, we praise Him. But we are not afraid of him. We love him and perfect love casts out all fear. That is why we seek the Lord to have contact with him. Without this our soul pines, our heart loses its joy, life returns again to uneasiness. But contact with God brings peace. The spiritual power is there only as we have a good contact with God. It is great, we see God when we look to Christ, and as we see his face in all the graphic imagery of Scripture, as the mind focuses upon him, then love, the love of Christ draws us to him and pervades our being.

Just being a believer does good to others about us

Then there is infinite love, so that as we are in contact with God in sweet communion, that love spills over for others to be blessed. I recall a serviceman in the Royal Air Force on a Station in England who was such a person. It is not what he said, but his presence had this quality which everyone seemed to recognise, a communicative kindness that uplifted people and made them feel that it was directed to them. There was another believer, an old Christian when I was a young boy in Aultbea. We were so happy as children when she would invite us into her house. There was such a lovely spirit about her. She was so gentle; we never got a row from her; it seemed that she had an inexhaustible supply of grace. We never knew if she was very smart, or articulate in spiritual truths. God gives his grace to each one in a different way. Just being with her, and it was not just for the candies she always gave us, did us all good. We will never forget old Miss Urquhart the friend of children, who showed the Christ-like love to children, sometimes a bit elusive in the church's fellowship. The gentle Christian lived alone in her house covered with ivy with the blue - framed dormer windows, sitting there above the road, overlooking the salmon rich waters of the river joining Loch Maree (The loch of Saint Maol -Rudha, a disciple of St Columba of the Celtic church). And when we come in to the finishing line and merge with the unseen hosts, who are already in glory, our hope is that we will also be with her.

David gives us a precedent for keeping in contact with God, our Redeemer. He loved the Lord and as we love him more and more, we will rejoice even when we have happy carefree times, and joy will fill our hearts, as Christ desired for his disciples.

That leads us to think of continuity in our new life-style.

We can never presume upon God. Any presumption, or taking God for granted, is sin. It is self-defeating and self-destructive. It contradicts the nature of true religion. Our therapeutic communion with God in Christ implies a living and continuous faith. Faith is not like a light switch that we put on when we need it; it is not dead when we are not praying or speaking as it were, on the phone to God. There are many of God's choicest people who are absorbed in doing his will, giving out, serving the Lord, by selfless involvement in his church. But there is continuity in their communion with God.

Faith in its working clothes

We are called to be servants of the Lord, to do his bidding, to carry messages of his love, even a word in season to those in distress. God is using people who have themselves tasted that he is gracious, to build up his church. When you see people doing God's will, serving the Lord by serving other people, you are seeing one of the wonders of the world, **faith in its working clothes**. And his church is made up of people who know the love of Christ that passeth knowledge. Therefore there must be continuity.

Carrying the torch for Christ

We are in a relay team in history. The torch has been handed over to us in our generation. We are called to carry it, as we run our race until we in turn hand it on to the next. What a glorious calling with which you are called. What an envious privilege to be called the chosen of God, and the children of God who are redeemed by the Blood of Christ. Let us be faithful to death and we shall receive a crown of life. Let nothing severe our connection with heaven and the Lord who called us. Let us prove we are his chosen ones, by our **constancy** in his service and the **continuity** we maintain in our witness to his redeeming love. God's love to us, not only changes life for us, but it changes life for those about us. Listen to St Paul as he expresses this ongoing witness to God's grace.

> *And grieve not the holy Spirit of God, whereby ye are sealed unto the day of redemption.*
> *Let all bitterness, and wrath, and anger and clamour, and evil speaking, be put away from you, with all malice:*
>
> *And be ye kind one to another, tenderhearted, forgiving one another, even as God for Christ's sake hath forgiven you.*

(Ephesians 4: 30 -32)

Continuity means that our testimony is something far greater than a three week wonder, or a flash message of a momentary faith, as a result of a need crisis that drives us to think of God as a last resort. But the great thing is that continuity is also the life-style of choice for us now. God so changes us that our souls desire him. And now we willingly continue in the life of his grace. We are now on the road of life where there is no end, but glory over the horizon of our vision. No longer does the soul wither in hopelessness, ever looking for short-term diversions to hide its sense of being crushed by fear. Now it is alive with an irrepressible power that makes you feel confident that you can face anything.

Calling on the true God

Then there is that connecting link of prayer. It must be to the God of Abraham, of Isaac and of Jacob, the God and Father of our Lord and Saviour Jesus Christ, the God who is of purer eyes than to behold iniquity, the God who is slow to anger and plenteous in mercy, the God who is just in all his ways, whose love shines out like light in darkness in wisdom power and holiness. That is the God you are to call upon, for He is the only Creator and Redeemer, able to renew, to remake, to build again, to release from debt, to pay for liberty, to vanquish the enemies of our souls - whose resources can never be exhausted, and whose compassions fail not.

I tell you this, Just you whisper to him. And I'll tell you more, and this is just the common experience of ten thousand thousand and tens of thousands, who make their journey through the years on the road to Sion. When in distress, you call upon God; you wait for him and be still. You may well hear a voice say to you, Is that you David? Is that you Mary? Is that you Jim? Is that you Catherine? The effect is just as Scripture records, *Hear and your soul shall live.* (Isaiah 55:3)

That, my friend, is enough to make your soul leap for joy. You have heard God speaking to you. What more could anyone want, God the Lord, Eternal Love who has the whole world in his hands, that he has bothered with you, although you have been deserted by all you friends! Do not be surprised at the release of tension in you, right through your whole being. Do not let anything restrain you as your heart becomes so full, that you break down in tears, yes, so that you cannot speak to anyone, only the love words of a soul that embraces its Saviour.

Keeping in touch with God

Hear what He says to you. *To his folk he'll speak peace.* The release of all your tensions and the answer to all your woes is his special and exclusive work. Try this, and in the continuing contact, say to God, I want to keep in touch with you always, day and night, in life in death, for evermore. Quote his word and his promise given to the disciples as he was parted from them in his physical return to glory,

> *and, lo, I am with you alway, even unto the end of the world.*

(St Matthew 28 : 20)

Conclusion

Now we come to the conclusion of our devotional thoughts on this song of the morning. But the conclusion is not the end. We go on like the Psalmist until at last our journey is ended, and our work is done. Our lives here are made up of so many threads, that are being woven into God's pattern for us, simultaneously. We think there will be a lot of loose ends; so much appears incomplete, so much unfinished. How glorious that whenever a child of faith is called home to his or her Saviour, the life is complete. Why is that so? Yes, because of the Finished work of Christ who is all in all. Through him we are made perfect, so that we are ready. We put off the working clothes of our witness in this life.

Then we will be dressed in his righteousness for the ongoing sequence of the immortal experiences. In these we shall walk with him in white; we shall see his face; we shall sing his praises; we shall sit at his banqueting table; we shall be led forth in peace; we shall be kings and priests unto God; we shall serve him, even the Lord of glory who is the Lamb of God that taketh away the sin of the world; we shall serve him day and night, for he, even the Lord Jesus is the sun that gives light to the renewed universe in the dimension of the spirit.

> *And there shall be no night there; and they need*
> *no candle, neither light of the sun; for the Lord*
> *God giveth them light; and they shall reign for*
> *ever and ever.*

> (Revelation 22:5)

That will be the last morning, when the redeemed awake in glory. Why should not this psalm which we sing here also be sung there, where there is no night of sorrow, no shedding of tears into our pillow, no queue of fears waiting their turn to agitate us! Then like, David *we will be satisfied when we awake in his likeness.* (Psalm17:15)

Take this psalm; make it yours now so that you become a **winner even now**, triumphing over every adversity, overcoming every enemy without and every fear within. Let John in the last chapter of Revelation lead us in our thoughts of this life's sequel, for those who live by faith in the Son of God, speaking to the church through the ages.

> *And behold I come quickly; and my reward is*
> *with me, to give every man according as his*
> *work shall be.*

> *I am Alpha and Omega, the beginning and the*
> *end, the first and the last.*

> *Blessed are they that do his commandments,*
> *that they may have right to the tree of life, and*
> *may enter in through the gates into the city.*

And the Spirit and the bride say, Come. And let him that heareth say, Come. And let him that is athirst come, And whosover will, let him take the water of life freely.

Even so, come, Lord Jesus.

Psalm 39

I said, I will take heed to my ways, that I sin not with my tongue: I will keep my mouth with a bridle, while the wicked is before me.

I was dumb with silence; I held my peace, even from good; and my sorrow was stirred.

My heart was hot within me, while I was musing, my heart burned: then spake I with my tongue.

Lord make me to know mine end, and the measure of my days, what it is; that I may know how frail I am.

And now Lord, what wait I for? my hope is in thee.

Deliver me from all my transgressions: make me not the reproach of the foolish.

Remove thy stroke away from me: I am consumed by the blow of thy hand.

Hear my prayer, O Lord, and give ear unto my cry; hold not thy peace at my tears: for I am a stranger with thee, and a sojourner, as all my fathers were.

O spare me, that I may recover strength, before I go hence, and be no more.

The Rock and the Rabbit

I met a young man one day as I walked over the rocky, treeless hillside of an island in Out-Skerries, lying to the north of Scotland. The young man had a gun, and was hunting for rabbits. I still see it all happen as I recall it after many years. As he pointed the gun at a stone not far from him, I felt like shouting, "What do you mean by doing that?, The bullet will rebound?" But at that moment the grey-brown stone moved. It moved fast, leaping with instant energy.

Of course, I was mistaken. It was not a stone, but a rabbit. As the young man approached, the rabbit decided to 'sit tight', to become as still as a stone, rather than take to its heels. Sometimes this works. 'Sit tight' is a tactic followed in soldiering. It is also the advice often given by a lawyer. 'Sit tight;' the police call out 'Freeze;' and God tells us when we are in straits, 'Be still'. But you are interested in what happened to the rabbit. The fact is that the young man's gun was a rifle with just one tiny .22 mm bullet, not a shot-gun which can hardly miss at close range. It seemed impossible, but the brave little creature did not fall back dead, but bounded off over the bare hill, zig-zagging almost as if it was air-borne, until it vanished into a safe refuge beyond our sight.

I tell you this because I can never forget it, and it seems to illustrate something about our lives. We try answers which have merit in them or at least appear to have. They can work in certain circumstances but not in all circumstances. They can work for certain relationships but not for all relationships. Remember the rabbit decided to 'sit tight'. But the tactic nearly cost him his life. He was confronted by a very sharp-eyed young man, who by the way was also a great lover of animals and birds and was elected as the school naturalist. He enriched the education of the island children with many stories of God's creatures.

Now, we all are confronted with God at one time or another, though not all in the same way, nor at the same time. This is it. We are all individuals, and God deals with us individually. In Psalm 39, we have a man who is caught in a predicament. His tactic is like that of the rabbit, to 'sit tight'. He says it himself,

> **I said, I will take heed to my ways, that I sin**
> **not with my tongue: I will keep my mouth**
> **with a bridle**

But the ruse did not work. Though he was as still as a stone, though he was as quiet as a mouse, this did not prove to be the right answer.

You see, as a psychological expedient this could work, just as Transcendental Postures may help in the disciplining of the person in human relationships. But when it comes to man's essential relationship to God, the trouble is deeper. It is within. Listen to this man David as he describes the failure of this expedient.

> **My heart was hot within me: while I was**
> **musing, the fire burned**

It seems a contradiction for Scripture itself recommends this tactic as we see in that great Psalm 46. But the quotation must include the whole recommendation which is "Be st*ill, and know that I am God*". You see in this answer which we are given here, there is the suspicion of humanist sufficiency; that here is a gospel of human potential. Do this and you can even deceive God. The God of all knowing; the God who is th*e discerner of the thoughts and intents of the heart. (*Hebrews 4:12) He is God Jehovah, proclaimed through the prophets and identified with Jesus of Nazereth, as the Christ, the Risen Son of Man, who spoke in the apocalyptic vision to John:

And all the churches shall know that I am he,
which searcheth the reins and hearts.

(Revelation 2:23)

Hear David articulating this answer which fails, in being caught out by God, for you and me. His resolution not to sin was powerless. You see, the will to perform, cannot operate when the heart is not at peace. The potential of man lies in what God can do through man, not what man can do through God. That sounds a paradox. But even the faith of St Paul who said *I can do all things through Christ is* valid only because it presupposes that *Christ strengtheneth him.* (Philip 4:13) Remember the rabbit, will you; just think of it. Here was a confrontation with one who could not be deceived, for whom a ruse or a posture would not work.

How much more true in our relations with God. An outward posture, and even an inward resolution not to sin has a powerlessness about it which betrays our own inner agony. We are not our own redeemers. We have not the ability to deal with our own spiritual troubles. We would like to think otherwise. There is a kind of kick-back of excitement, of feeling good, of self-congratulation in finding an answer ourselves that seems to work. And there is obviously a place and a time for the resolution **I will keep my mouth with a bridle.** But when it is 'heart - trouble', when God is involved, and when he is looking upon us, there is no expedient or ruse of our own devising, that can deceive him, even though we be 'still as a stone.'

If it were only known, inside many people the heart is like a furnace. The outward mask and the apparently confident posture is a self-deception. Like David's case there can be no hope for us in our spiritual dilemmas in bringing to them our own solutions. But we praise God that David did not leave it at that, but went on to tell us of another tactic which in its nature was active and positive, and therefore full of promise.

Prayer:

> Lord show me how weak I am, that I can do nothing without thee, that even my good resolutions of will, can never be the answer for the troubles of my heart. For thou only can treat the broken heart.

Memory:

> **With silence I as dumb became**
> **I did myself restrain**
> **From speaking good; but then the more**
> **increased was my pain.**

Trying another tack

One of the characteristics of freedom is that people have a degree of choice. Choice in what they eat, what they work at, what kind of life they live. It goes without saying that freedom has its perils. It also goes without saying that when a person abuses that freedom of choice, and suffers the consequences, the last person he blames is himself.

Listening to a commentator last evening on the radio, whose hobby was sky-diving - the art of dropping out of an aeroplane, in risky parachute jumps - with all the latent perils, I noted that he said, 'Most accidents take place when people act outside of safety rules.' The accident factor incidentally was only .6 per cent, and that, due mainly to the non-opening of the primary parachute. And even then, for this eventuality, there was a safety cord to open the emergency chute, provided the flier kept his head.

Choice is a great value which gives freedom quality but it must be exercised within the rules. And this is more imperative in our spiritual dealings with God than in any localised sphere of our lives. But you see the point, the onus or the blame must lie at our door, when things go wrong - not all the blame - no, there may be many other factors which can be identified as causal. And even in the last resort God himself can be seen in the picture in his permissive will. But if it comes to that, what a glorious progression in our perception that we should perceive the hand of God in our lives, the God of all creation and all grace, who is *slow to anger and plenteous in mercy.* (Psalm 103:8)

We noted that David tried one tack. He thought that he could solve his 'heart trouble, his spiritual problem, which was affecting his whole life as it usually does, **by being still.** He was going to be a good fellow; he would not sin; he would pretend he was like a stone, like the rabbit caught out by the hunter. Doing nothing cannot be an answer. That's a negative, and often a justifiable indictment of religious practice. David found his trouble continued to burn in his heart like a furnace.

So that David, to turn to another dimension of analogy, was forced to try another tack. I've seen it, you probably have seen it too, yachts or sailing dinghies beating against the wind trying one tack to the left and one to the right. I recall watching the Clyde Regatta with a hundred yachts, big and small, from large old Fyfe designed yawls to the swift McGruer Piper Class, - I say watching this, you could see the yachts, holding on to a starboard tack as long as they could, trying to make as much windward progress as possible, only to find that they had to tack to port or come to grief on the shore of Bute. What a fate!

But we are looking to David, because he represents to us the reasonable man, one who furthermore was no stranger to God, though sin, his sin had estranged him from God. My friend this is a 'must'. It is pathetic to hold on to our own ways, and our own devices when all indications point to their foolishness.

Refusing to admit we went wrong

In a boatyard a man was putting panes of glass into the sides and front of the wheelhouse frames of a lovely mahogany launch. He had taken the exact measurements and had the glass panes cut accordingly. There was no doubt about it, the panes were cut exactly to the dimensions of the window frames. You see, he was not a shipwright, he was a skilled marine engineer. He was used to working to exact measurements and did not know the allowances to be made when working with both glass and wood. He knew the rule that allowances had to be made for fitting metal to metal but he thought - I heard him say this - that in working with wood there was no need to make any allowance.

The snag is that he was fitting glass panes into wood frames. There were eight panes of glass. A group of well-wishers were there in the boatyard passing the time of day and watching at the time. For Duncan was a popular man. There was a crack as the first pane was pressed into the frame. The fitting was tight. Did my good friend stop to consider? Oh no. Pane after pane was put in, crack after crack faithfully followed. He would not stop until all but the last glass were in the frames. No one said a word. All knew my friend had a very strong sense of pride and no one could let on in any way that anything was wrong, or that somehow he had made a mistake. Hope still burned at least dimly that somehow he would be vindicated at last. But no, even the last pane of glass, as it was pressed in to the puttied frame gave the now familiar crack. At that point all of the bystanders melted away from the scene of humiliation. Though no word was said, our great friend had 'lost face' and he now knew it.

You see how pride prevented my friend from admitting he had made a mistake. He could have had an eighth of an inch ground off the other panes of glass after the first cracked, or the slot in the frames slightly worked with a sharp chisel. But now, all the panes were fitted into the wheelhouse and without exception each had its own little crack in a corner.

God has given each one of us freedom, not to abuse it but to use it so that we will turn to him, but so often our pride prevents us from admitting even to ourselves that our life does not work when we go by our own insights. Hear the prophet in his lament for Israel as he saw its stubborn pride.

> *Cast away from you all your transgressions, whereby ye have transgressed; and make you a new heart and a new spirit: for why will ye die, O house of Israel.*

(Ezekiel 18:31)

A homing pigeon is released a thousand miles away, though it is of great value, because its owner knows that it will make its way back home. Thus God gives freedom, so that we have alternatives. This does not infer that he casts us off, that he does not care for us or think that we are worthless. Rather he lets us go, to prove that we are his, when like the homing pigeon, we return to him.

Turning to the Lord

Thus David shows us this alternative which by the way was not easy. Turning to God and repenting is humbling. Admitting that we went wrong, that we took a wrong turning, that we sinned, that we had all the answers, is never easy. But if only we knew the tender loving-kindness of our heavenly Father and the gentle way he deals with us, we would not delay in turning to him in confession and supplication. This comprises five positive pleas which we take to God in prayer.

To be still as we are commanded in Psalm 46 is good, but not enough. Faith is not passive. Being still relates to disposition, and that is a subject in itself that certainly has to be considered. When we look to the horizon, using a telescope, we stand still. But what is the profit in doing this though we stand still all day. We have to lift up the telescope to our eyes. We have to focus the lens. We have to use common sense and look in the right direction. Faith acts and focuses on God in a similar manner. The positive element is *and know that I am God.*

Thus in the case of David's new tack, we notice these five positive features as we see them in Psalm 39.

First, A plea for knowledge

> **Lord, make me to know mine end, and the measure of my days, what it is; that I may know how frail I am.**

Try this. It is a prayer to God. It is positive. Send it like a telegram to heaven. Shout it out in the storm that has overtaken you. God will hear, make no mistake. Just ask for your position. Of course implicit in this is a confession that you have not got all the answers; that you have fears; that your assurance in yourself has faded out and is in tatters, like a sail that has been blown out by a squall of wind. But also explicit in this is the proof that you have faith, even though weak, even as if it is a last desperate try. And God will never give anyone up, just because he was the last person to whom the sinner came for an answer.

Second, A hope directed to God
David says:

> **What am I waiting for. My hope is in God. Deliver me from all my transgressions. Make me not the reproach of the foolish.**

One effect of our transgressions against the law of God is that we incur the derision of the world, so that we are the laughing stock of others. Sadly some who profess to be the people of God, join in and laugh at a believer when he is down. This had particular pain for David. The fact is that the world gloats if a righteous man strays into the paths of sin. Yet he cannot tell the world, 'Look, I am just human; I'm just like yourselves. I'm just an ordinary person'.

The world will just not accept this. And neither can he accept it himself, because at heart, he knows that he is different, that God has touched him with his spirit and given him blessings that make him the object of Divine love and the recipient of God's forgiveness. He has tasted the living waters of heaven; he belongs to Christ the Saviour; he is not his own, and he is not of the world, though in the world.

Thus if he strays out of the paths of righteousness, he is rightly the object of reproach and mockery. Do you see the point? Are you in this predicament? Your only hope is in God. But what a hope you have if it is in God! For this is not wishful thinking, but effectual prayer.

Lord ..... deliver me from all my transgressions

The result is that God comes into the picture in the positive action of the Spirit. Then you are like a boat that has had to battle against a strong off-shore wind. When it gets into the lee of the land, and the higher the land is the better, the crew relax and rejoice and make a meal, for they are safe, although the wind rises to hurricane force. It is no different when we seek shelter under the protection of our God and the redemptive atoning provision of Christ. Now we are free from the reproach of the world. We have a safe haven to rest until duty calls to move on, in obedience to God's will for us. Even though you suffer and are mocked as a Christian, it is good to remember, that there will be many well-wishers in heaven and earth who will rejoice as you find y*ourself* again and lay yourself at the feet of your Redeemer.

There is a cynicism in the world that makes hope itself a futile illusion even when we think it has substance. Asking one time at Stornoway airport, if there was a vacant seat on the aircraft, during a seamen's strike which cancelled the ferry to

The mainland, I was told, 'What a hope'. You've heard this too. That is the sum of scepticism for you and me, when we look for answers to our spiritual problems in any other source but in God himself. Do not be fooled by the humanist state that chokes up our society with all kinds of counsellors, trained in disciplines, without spiritual knowledge of the soul. In a very real and practical way they also choke up the ordinary citizen with higher taxes to pay for their sinecures.

But when a person turns to heaven, there is no need to look to the skies, there is no need to start musing, whether he will be in heaven or his neighbor be in hell. Jesus told Peter that such speculation was an irrelevance. Rather we are given a sign of looking to God in this positive way of believing. Then our hope is in him, and like David, we will to turn to study God's word, given to us *as a lamp to our feet and a light to our path.* (Psalm119: 105) And in the New Testament it is spelt out for Jew and Gentile who merge together in the acknowledgment of the promised Messiah, Jesus of Nazareth, and the Eternal Son of God, as the hope for the world.

> *Which hope we have as an anchor of the soul, both sure and stedfast, which entereth into that within the veil.*
>
> *Whither the forerunner is for us entered, even Jesus, made an high priest for ever after the order of Melchisedec.* (Hebrews 6:19)

Third, We see David asks God not to chastise him

David says in his prayer to God **Remove thy stroke away from me.** Clearly God was involved in the trouble that David was going through. Further David was aware that God had rebuked him. A rebuke from one who loves us, can be implicit in the fact that he sees us sinning, without his saying a word of rebuke. If we are his, when we realise that he has seen us, it is enough to rend our hearts and cover us with shame. Is that not true to life! Anyone who loves us does not need to come to us with a whip. Only that we know that he has seen us, brings the agony of rebuke. Take away the situational ethic which incorporates being as*hamed of ourselves* and we go a long way in denying the strategy of the redemptive and restoring process by which God's children are reinstated in their Father's House.

Is it not true that when we are ashamed, we bow our heads? But we need not keep our heads down, like misbehaving schoolboys. We have a God whose great delight is in mercy, and who in Christ and the efficacy of the Cross, has enough and to spare to forgive and pardon all our sins. Look up and look to Christ. We say, Look up to Christ; if your hope is in God, you are justified. And my friend if you just cannot lift up your head, do what David did in his agony. Go to a quiet place, beside a dyke on a Highland croft, in an old gun-pit on a military airfield, or if it has to be that you are in a crowded building, turn your head into your pillow and pour out your heart before the Lord, and say,

Remove thy stroke away from me

Remember, say it to God. Others may look lightly on your sin or treat it as a joke. They may even rejoice in your falling. David could tell you this. How different to those who are part of the circle of true believers, who grieve when Christ's name is offended, who suffer because they are members of the one body of Christ and are therefore hurt by your injury!

But we must go on. Who said that we can do nothing! Prayer is powerful. God in the intercessory role of our Risen Lord pleads that we may be kept from evil. What a thought! Already God in his healing, forgiving love is waiting to be gracious, to restore us to reinstate us. He is waiting for us to come to the throne of his grace, with our tears, but more than just our tears, with contrite hearts.

Pray again and again. Pray often. So that the secret place of prayer will be sweet to you and so that you will be so addicted to it that you cannot live without it. We are to put our body into it, like Ezra praying to God before the congregation. Do not be afraid to put all your strength into it, remember, put heart and soul and mind and strength into your prayers like all the mandatory requirements of our spiritual calling. Wrestle with God. Put all you've got into it, though it bring sweat and tears. Just keep on praying to God. Do not let him go without his blessing. For your hope is in God alone.

Therefore say, again and again **O Lord, remove thy stroke away from me.** Let that prayer out, again and again. Cry out. Do you know that God is very human? He likes to be implored. Scores of folk have been conned into using instant prayer all the time, like instant coffee and minute rice. Of course there is a place for the instant prayer but only in emergency. The ordered Christian life incorporates prayer, woven into the thinking processes of our mind. It is not enough to leave our prayers in bundles at the Door of Mercy, because we are in a hurry or because we have so many things to do in this busy life. God wants to see us ourselves; he wants to find us on the steps of penitence outside the Door of Mercy. He wants to lift up our heads, to dry our tears. He wants to take us in, and embrace us with his love and heal us with his righteousness. He wants to hear our prayers in person so that he can answer us directly and anoint us with his Spirit.

David said that it was vain to wait in a passive way, even

for God. So he went into action. Prayer is dynamic spiritual action. He got up and went to God in person with his prayer. It may well be that he had to keep on praying. But one thing is sure. He did not just jot down a hurried note and leave it at the doorstep of the Throne of Mercy. He waited to address God in person. My friend this is a must.

You have a spiritual problem! Then scrap the instant stuff whether it be from an evangelist or an ecologist. And do not worry if folk think you unChristian, when you prostrate yourself on the floor - you better do it in private, repeat, repeat, repeat this positive prayer, morning after morning night after night day after day.

Remove thy stroke away from me: I am consumed by the blow of thy hand.

It is regrettable but there is no smooth instant stuff here. Go somewhere else for that. Also remember you yourself must wait in person with your prayer. Of course that is asking a lot, when you think how busy you are, even possibly on church business. It is amazing how many people are so busy on church business, that they have no time to give for the health of their souls. But God does not make exceptions unless there are very good reasons. He treats every one equitably or fairly, without prejudice to any. But the premise of all help from God must be our prayers. The promises, the blessings, the grace, all the glorious things that God can do can be granted only to those who wait on the Lord. So remember, you just cannot leave a message. You must wait in person, be you priest, punter or president.

But you may object, If I go on repeating the same prayer, it will become mechanical and monotonous. You have a point there. It can become mechanical. In fact there is a possibility that your prayer will lose all meaning and end up as rather funny jargon. This is often an apparently justifiable observation which those who are indifferent to God use as an excuse for not approaching God themselves. The prayers of others appear as jibberish and just possibly they are justified, - that is in their own eyes and even in the view of sympathetic friends. But in no way are they justified in God's sight until and when they appropriate the righteousness of God through faith in Jesus Christ.

The little boy who wanted out

A little schoolboy wanted to leave the classroom. The infant mistress had her back to the class, as she carefully, with different coloured chalk, wrote words on the blackboard. The little boy raised his hand, and at the same time called, Please Ma'am can I get out - the usual form of request to visit the washroom. This was in a little school in the Highlands of Scotland in 1937. The little boy had a very soft voice so that the teacher did not seem to hear. Or maybe she was waiting to finish her writing on the board. At any rate there was no response from the teacher and the boy kept on repeating, 'Please Ma'am can I get out'. 'Please Ma'am can I get out'. At last just as the teacher turned round to respond to him, he realised that his request had unthinkingly changed to Plea*se mamma canibalout*, or *Please Mam can I bale out.* He blushed with confusion at his mistake. But when he saw the look in the teacher's kindly face, he knew that she understood. I'll never forget the look in Miss McCann's eyes. She seemed to see my agony, and did not expose me to mortification before the rest of the class. It is true that sometimes a coherent prayer may indeed tire our lips. But God will not give up on a soul under any circumstances if he waits on the steps of penitence or at the door of Mercy.

Thus we learn from David a way in which this devaluing of our prayer is prevented. We see his prayer though positive changes to another note. It is still prayer in action. It is still positive. It is powerful. It is somewhat like a wrestler changing his position, relaxing for a moment his grip, in order to get a better hold on his opponent. Thus we note this

Fourth, A plea for God to hear him

This is the variation that he introduces in his prayer:

Hear my prayer, O Lord and give ear unto my cry...

Now this is a note that is often used by David in many of the Psalms. It is like music when it is heard in heaven. Remember David was musical and a master at playing the harp. We cannot all be musical or play musical instruments with skill in our fingers. But the words we take to God in prayer can equal any musical chord or harmony. After all, music is the harmony of different sounds; words are also the vocal expression from the human being, comprising controlled emisions of acoustic vibrations. Thus a singer is a human musical instrument and singing praises with the human voice must ultimately be the greatest music in the world. Thus we can all use this note among others,

Hear my prayer Lord, and give ear unto my cry

It is heard in heaven. It is a plaintive note; it is full of pathos, beseeching God to hear. Clearly the suppliant is in trouble, trouble of the heart, but this prayer is full of promise. How can we say that with such certainty? Because the prayer is made to the Almighty, Jehovah, the *Creator of the ends of the earth, who fainteth not nor is weary; there is no searching of his understanding.* (Isaiah 40:26) He calls God **his Lord.** It is like Thomas when he saw the Risen Jesus with the wound in his side and the print of the nails in his hands, he bowed before Jesus, and said, My *Lord and my God.* (John 20:28)

This is a note to strike in our prayers often as we lift them to God. Watch a pianist as the fingers flit across the keyboard. He is not afraid to use the key to repeat the chords. It is just like that when this note is sounded.

My Lord and my God

This use of language strikes a chord in the ear of God. It is as if in Heaven the dialogue is something like this. 'There is someone on the phone.'

'What is he saying?' Is it that one who has slavish fear, who we often have calling up when he is in physical trouble, but never is aware of his spiritual plight?'

Or 'Is it that one whom heaven is tapping, as he communicates with the prince of darkness, to hurt one of our chosen ones who is permitted to go through the fire for a season?'.

No. Alright who is it? David, you say, our own David whom we knew since he prayed to us as a shepherd boy and now is king of Israel. What is David wanting now? Of course, he is on the prayer phone every day, writing his commentary for the soul in its journey of faith, in conflict, in joy, in sin, and salvation. What is he saying?'

'He is desperate, he's using that note again, the one we promised we would never ignore, the code words of heaven'.

Hear my prayer Lord, give ear unto my cry

Are you still there my friend? Do you realise what this means for you? Here is an answer which meets your greatest spiritual needs. It can be used by the believer and the non-believer. But remember God is not fooled by the charlatan. He discerns the thoughts and intents of the heart We are an open book before him and he reads the pages of our life history, the hidden writing even between the lines that tell the inside story of our motives and all the inner motions of our soul, behind the actions that are seen by the world about us.

It is as if there is an exchange in heaven itself; remember Christ is Risen and sitteth on the right hand of God, the Father Almighty, the advocate of sinners, making continual intercession for us. And only where the other half of the code corresponds to the message from the plaintiff, only then does it read as **genuine** before God.

What is the other half of the code? All we can say and we get this from Scripture is that *the Lord knows them that are his.* (2nd Timothy 2:19)

My sheep hear my voice, and I know them. (John 10:27)

It is not a matter of where they are. They may be well away from the paths of righteousness, like a ship heading across the Atlantic, which is driven off course by currents, storm, or human navigational error, or instrument error. Even as the ship still belongs to its owner and is precious to him, so the soul that has strayed far away off course, still belongs to Christ. He is Christ's by purchase, paid in full with all the privileges, won in the victory on Calvary's Cross. And Christ *saves to the uttermost, all that come unto him.* (Hebrews 7:25)

The power of Christ to redeem, to locate the lost, to restore, to rescue makes child's play of modern technology in the greatest demonstration of its wonders. But God uses technology for his purposes. God is not bigotted. There is nothing new under the sun, and we believe God encourages man to rediscover all the hidden secrets of his physical habitat. Then God makes use of all this in the communication necessary to bring salvation to the ends of the earth.

Even as the helicopter is used so often in the 20th century to airlift casualties from downed aircraft in inaccessible places like mountains or roadless forests, or stormy seas, or oil-rigs off Newfoundland or in the North Sea, so God can rescue those who call upon him wherever they may be. Since the 1990's, travellers on land or voyagers on the ocean know where they are, using satellites and their tiny Global Positioning System (GPS) unit. Predictably with the third millenium, millions will know within a few feet, their position on earth, on land or sea, by reading their GPS like a wristwatch. And who knows. There may be a dark side to this. Someone or some politico-social master may also know where everyone of us are at any time. What ominous possibilities for mass manipulation of a Hitler, all masked in the guise of advanced technology. Where then our boasted freedom? Instead, slavery.

The pitfalls of ill-use of technology

Who can imagine what is ahead, as the position of each human being is entered at birth into a central computer, and traced throughout the lifespan and potentially monitored. This can be for good or evil, for freedom or slavery. Here is potential for those engaged in power seeking, and its concomitant of fear and subservience in the populace.

This is an important point which must be stressed. We judge by where people are. This is human, but God does not judge as man judges. He judges not by sight of the eyes, but tri*es the reins* (Jeremiah 11:20) and the heart. For God, the question is not Where are they?, but Whose are they? And here is a mystery. You will find fault and say, So God will rescue only those that are his! Yes, that is right. But we are not given a list of those who belong to Christ, in this life. The Book of life will be opened in glory, the *Lamb's book of life* (Revelation 22:27) with all the names of the redeemed who were bought out of bondage to sin and purchased with the shed blood of Christ. But no one, no church, no bishop, no minister, no session, no ecclesiastical authority has a list of those who belong to Christ. That's a bombshell for the establishment, whether it likes it or not.

What possibilities for strangers, for great sinners like me, maybe for you as well. What encouragement for all who have no peace for their souls. For Jesus said *him that cometh unto me, I will in no wise cast out.* (John 6:37) All who call upon the Lord shall be saved. Hear both Peter and Paul affirming the breadth and length and height and depth of God's mercy and the bountiful riches of Christ, for all people.

Peter links great times for the church to the prophecy of Joel,

> *And it shall come to pass in the last days, saith*
> *God, I will pour my Spirit upon all flesh: and*
> *your sons and your daughters shall prophesy,*
> *and your young men shall see visions, and your*
> *old men shall dream dreams.* (Joel 2:28)

Thus you have the three, Joel, Peter and Paul making this glorious announcement to all who will,

> th*at whosoever shall call on the name of the*
> *Lord shall be saved.*
>
> (Acts 2:21); (Romans 10:13)

What breadth there is in the Gospel! It is not qualified, by historic identity, by ethnic preferences, by cultural exclusiveness.

> *For the same Lord over all is rich unto all that*
> *call upon him.*
>
> (Romans 10:12)

But now look at David. He is shown to us praying, striking the note of the penitent, the humble in heart, suffering what he believes to be the permissive will of God.

I was dumb, I opened not my mouth; because
thou didst it.

(verse 9)

We are encouraged to follow David's example. How easy it is to take offence when we think of the hard things that come our way, that appear indeed to be at least the permissive will of God. Then bitterness enters the soul and poisons the healing process of the spirit. We must pray to the Lord, striking the positive note, ascribing the power to God, to alleviate our suffering and bring light to our darkness. And our prayers must cor**respond** to our hearts. No objective requests are accepted in heaven without corresponding to the disposition of the humble and the penitent heart. We are told this from David's experience.

> *The Lord is nigh unto them that are of a broken*
> *heart; and saveth such as be of a contrite spirit.*
> (Psalm 34:18)

What then? What if God as it were does come to the phone and listens? What is he going to hear after this *Lord hear me, Lord hear me* ?

Faith however small goes on to other **positives.** David called upon God to help him, and now he asks God

Fifth, To renew him, to make him strong again

> **O spare me that I may recover strength,**
> **before I go hence, and be no more**

That's it, he wants to be renewed. He wants to be strong again. He wants to get back his spiritual health. He has come to the right place, the spiritual clinic for souls in trouble, and to a God whose business it is to make people whole, and to maintain their health, by treating them for all the knocks and wear and tear on life's highway. Is this not that which we all need, a turn-around where people of all kinds leave the pseudo-physicians of this world and come to the great **physician of souls** for healing and redeeming!

Here is a prayer which makes this case, whether it be David's or yours or the case of *whosoever will,* - sorry no lists of Heaven are given on earth - another 'hit' as it were for glory. It is not that David knows yet. But in fact even as his prayer is monitored on the screen of God's omniscience, and as it is articulated in the language of the broken heart, so it is accepted before the Throne of Grace, and the power to answer with the saving grace of heaven is already engaged to heal and to strengthen.

It is strange, but God is looking for people with broken

hearts. Why on earth do not more come to him, when you consider all the grief and pain of mankind? Why do so many go to quacks, to pseudo-healers, to spiritual tricksters who claim they have a special link with God?

We speak of wire-tapping in the commercial world, where businesses eavesdrop on rivals, in order to get the secrets of their processes in products that are a success. It is also true in the sphere of the spirit. There is wire-tapping by rivals to the kingdom of our Lord. Those who are Christ's, do business with heaven; they have the secret of obtaining spiritual power with God. They know the power of prayer. False christs, and false guides within the spiritual realm want the secrets of heaven. The idea is as old as witchcraft. King Saul went to the witch of Endor, and there was conjured up for him, a picture of Samuel, who had died. (1st Samuel 28: 7 - 16) It was when Saul had lost his communion with God, that he turned to a sorcerer.

What a warning for all of us! We are surrounded by charlatans, rivals to Christ, who operate in cults, that deceive multitudes and lead to their destruction. They operate as pseudo-saviours, even using the name of Jesus, yet are really thieves of Christ's credentials and the powers they claim do not come from heaven but from Satan. We read of Simon the sorcerer in Samaria, who was baptized along with others, through the preaching of Philip. We are told that they as yet had no signs of the spiritual presence of the Holy Spirit. But this Simon coveted the gifts of apostleship as he saw them in the work of the apostles and the power that Christ had bestowed upon them. He offered money to get this power. We are told how Peter rebuked him and called him to truly repent, saying.

Thy money perish with thee, because thou hast
thought that the gift of God may be purchased
with money. Thou has neither part nor lot in
this matter: for thy heart is not right in the

sight of God. Repent therefore of this thy wickedness, and pray God, if perhaps the thought of thine heart may be forgiven thee. For I perceive that thou art in the gall of bitterness and in the bond of iniquity.

(Acts 8:20 - 23)

What a great Gospel of redeeming love that still presents hope to those who have to do with spiritual evil. There is a pathos in the answer given to Peter. *Pray ye to the Lord for me, that none of these things which ye have spoken come upon me.* (ibid verse 24)

We know only in part and cannot know in the absolute sense. The Gospel of Christ is an open revelation as opposed to a secret cult and is cosmic in the net of magnetic love, drawing men and women from the uttermost, to Christ. It is easy to tune in to the wavelengths of heaven, short, medium or long and even very high frequency, and so pretend that one is on speaking terms with God, and claim Divine power to deceive other people.

I often listen to the world radio network. Several stations broadcast in English, apart from the British Broadcasting Service. The latter is unique in its excellence and impartiality - with rare exceptions. Other stations appear to be the same, but after a few moments, it becomes clear that they are not the BBC. That is reasonable, but some stations, especially before the rending of the Iron Curtain over Eastern Europe, on both sides of the fence projected political ideology and slanted the news so that facts were presented to convey a particular impression to the listener. There are many combinations of facts, of inclusion and omission which give a different answer without an untruth being told. Truth has a ring about it that reflects integrity, proven integrity, historical integrity, seasoned in time and tested over the centuries. And truth, even in what we term the secular sense, or the authentic scientific sense, is not divorced from the spiritual norms of our moral life, even as the moral is inseparable from the spiritual.

Where does that lead us except to the Scriptural premise of existence itself as inseparable from faith. Faith believes before it sees. Faith in falsehood comes to disillusionment and sorrow. Faith directed to heaven brings the promises of God to the door of our heart. God is well pleased in this and the effect of his good-will is that we can live life abundantly. All does not happen at once. But through the *once and for all* sacrifice of Christ, we grow like new-born children, through adolescence to maturity. David was already a long-time believer in God, yet we are looking here at one of the phases or experiences of his life of faith, one in which we see prayer as central. There is no praise in this Psalm, but wait my friend and you will hear of that later and that will lift up your heart too so that your soul will rejoice like David for *what the Lord hath done.*

Hear Scripture:

For without faith, it is impossible to please him (God) : for he that cometh to God must believe that he is, and that he is the rewarder of them that diligently seek him.

(Hebrews 11: 6)

Here is a prayer of faith. Faith looks to God. Faith calls upon God. Faith is mighty, even though it be found in the setting of weakness. When we pray in faith, we take the Bible off the shelf, we open its pages, we read the Word. But only as we believe, and bring these promises to God along with our needs, only then does expectation of hope rise in our hearts. This will never fail, God just cannot let people down; it is a contradiction of his nature. He is full of compassion and his love for us is measureless, and in Christ his resources of divine healing are like a great canal, the Suez or the Panama, giving access to his grace.

This prayer is indeed a human action, someone doing something about his troubles. He goes to God for a cure. And this is the prayer for you and me when we also are in trouble, so that we feel that God has laid a stroke upon us which has crushed us. But like Job we will say, *Though he slay me, yet I will trust in him.* (Job 13:15) We know that even when the chastisement of the Lord is upon us, this itself illustrates that he loves us. That is enough for me. What more do we want!

For whom the Lord loveth he chasteneth and scourgeth every son whom he receiveth.

(Hebrews 12:6)

And there is something else that the Lord's people can never forget. *While they were yet sinners Christ died for them,* and whatever they go through as the permissive will of God, can be blessed to them. For in their heart they know that any such visitation of hardship, and sorrow, is less than their iniquities deserve.

This prayer is a prayer for you. You have to do something. This is positive. Do not think God wants you to do nothing. **Being still** is not an excuse for doing nothing. It obviously will not get you anywhere spiritually. Being still is really only like a person with a telescope. He has to steady himself; he has stop moving as he lifts the telescope to his eye. But however steady he is, it is of no avail until he looks into the telescope, and in the steps of looking in the right direction, focussing the instrument for clarity, looking through the telescope he adjusts the lens to bring near the object he is looking for.

Follow David, in these five positive steps. The virtue in them lies in the fact that they are steps to the Throne of Grace and to the Room of Mercy and to the Door of Hope, even Christ the Lord. Just try this sequence in prayer. And when you ring up heaven, do not be put off by a delay. Do not hang up; give God a chance; he is testing you. He wants to make sure that **your heart coincides with the prayer**. When that is the case,

it is like the other half of the code coming together in heaven
and you will hear in due course God's answer.

Lord make me to know mine end
Deliver me from my transgression
Remove thy stroke from me
Hear my prayer, O Lord
Spare me that I may recover strength.

I said, I will look to my ways,
    lest with my tongue I sin:
In sight of wicked men my moth
    with bridle I'll keep in.

With silence I as dumb became.
I did myself restrain
From speaking good; but the more
    increased was my pain.

My heart within me waxed hot;
    and, while I musing was,
The fire did burn; and from my tongue
    these words I did let pass:

Mine end and measure of my days,
O Lord, unto me show
What is the same; that I thereby,
    my frailty well may know.

Lo, thou my days a handbreadth mad'st;
    mine age is in thine eye
As nothing: sure each man at best
    is wholly vanity.

And now, O Lord, what wait I for?
My hope is fixed on thee.
Free me from all my trespasses,
The fool's scorn make not me.

Dumb was I opening not my mouth,
Because this work was thine.
Thy stroke take from me; by the blow
    of thine hand I do pine.

Attend my cry, Lord, at my tears,
    and prayers not silent be:
I sojourn as my fathers all,
    and strangers am with thee.

O spare thou me that I my strength
    recover may again.
Before from hence I do depart,
    and here no more remain.

(Psalm 39   Scottish Psalter)

Father of peace, and God of love!
We own thy power to save,
That power by which our Shepherd rose
Victorious o'er the grave.

Him from the dead thou brought'st again
When by his sacred blood,
Confirmed and sealed for evermore
The eternal covenant stood.

O may thy spirit seal our souls,
And mould them to thy will,
That our weak hearts no more may stray,
But keep they precepts still;

That to perfection's sacred height
We nearer still may rise,
And all we think, and all we do,
Be pleasing in thy eyes.

Scottish Paraphrases
From Hebrews 13:20, 21

Psalm 41

Blessed is he that considereth the poor: the Lord will deliver him in the time of trouble.

The Lord will preserve him, and keep him alive; and he shall be blessed upon the earth: and thou wilt not deliver him unto the will of his enemies.

The Lord will strengthen him upon the bed of languishing: thou wilt make all his bed in his sickness.

I said, Lord be merciful unto me: heal my soul; for I have sinned against thee.

My enemies speak evil of me, When shall he die, and his name perish?

And if he come to see me, he speaketh vanity: his heart gathereth iniquity to itself; when he goeth abroad, he telleth it.

Yea, mine own familiar friend, in whom I trusted, which did eat of my bread, hath lifted up his heel against me.

A Faith that is Justified

This psalm begins with God's benediction upon those who give out or extend a helping hand in one way or another to the less fortunate. We tend to think that the less fortunate in life are the only ones that suffer. It seems strange, but it is nevertheless true, that often those who are touched with a spirit of humanity for others, are themselves visited with trouble, and here we are told that God promises to be their help. What follows from this fact is, that whatever prosperity may come to us in our lives, we all need God's grace. The very one who has compassion on others in their distress, is also the person who has increased sensitivity to the moral and spiritual presentations which surround us all, as Christ with his challenge confronts us in our minds and hearts.

The person who remembers the poor, who cannot insulate himself from the sufferings of others apparently, must also be strengthened. The very one who appears well-off and apparently completely happy, is often the one that is most in need of God's grace, just as the poor who have but the simplest food and the most humble dwelling, can go to bed at night with their loved ones round them, in peace and serenity.

Thus we see in this Psalm, a word in season for the rich, the affluent, the well-off, those who have no immediate struggle for their daily bread or the other reasonable requirements of life. There is no benediction, no blessing, no happiness stated here for those who are impervious to the needs of the less fortunate. But in the implied contrast, there is a wonderful attractiveness for those who have a sense of humanity and extend a helping hand to the needy. For those who use their means as conscious stewards of God's goodness for the aid of others less fortunate, there are unbounded returns. Some energetic entrepreneurs may be damned by contemporaries, as they grow rich in this world's goods. But some of these rich, after they have reached their goals, disburse their riches generously.

Clearly all judgements of people and their motives can be exploded and prove to be unjust. One thinks of the latest case even as I write, namely the case of Gates, the 'king' of the computer world and the Microsoft company. Having brought upon himself the stigma of ruthlessness and avarice, he has brought 'coals of fire down on the heads' of his critics by announcing a donation of one hundred million dollars for vaccinating children in developing countries. On the other hand in the cynical climate of the modern world, such could be considered expediency.

Another aspect of David's life is brought into the Psalm. It is inferred that this person of means who is actively concerned for the underprivileged, is experiencing trouble. He is distressed within himself, so that his whole disposition is affected, as well as his physical health. Clearly this person is vulnerable to the enmity of others. He takes to his bed.

Those who have resentments against him spread rumours that he has some venereal disease. And as we all know, when a rumour or some speculative idea gains currency, the public in general are somehow influenced to believe it as truth.

In the United States a distinguished physician, had a rumour spread about him that he was dying of AIDS. Almost overnight his patients melted away, his friends shunned him. After going through a terrible nightmare of pain and trouble, for over four years, only slowly things came back to normal, when it became clear that everyone were mistaken. The little fire kindled by a loose tongue, fuelled by resentment had caused a conflagration which nearly destroyed this man and his family. Listen to what they were saying about the man who wrote this Psalm,

All they that hate me whisper against me: against me do they devise hurt. An evil disease, say they cleaveth fast unto him.

(verse 7, 8)

Apart from rumours which can destroy anyone of us, there is a wide range of people who can identify with this psalm. It includes those who have sinned in some specific way, but who are contrite and humbly penitent before God. Listen to the psalmist,

'I said, Lord, be merciful unto me: heal my soul; for I have sinned against thee.'

(verse 4)

How very familiar the picture is, as we read human nature, unchanged after thousands of years and supposedly progressive civilization, and the leaven of God's love to us in the Gospel of Christ. Here is a man who has taken to his bed. He is confident that God will heal him,

The Lord will help him when he is sick, and restore him to health.

(verse 3) NEB

But in contrast to this confidence, there is almost a public attempt to wish him into the grave. Apart from his enemies who naturally do not wish him well and he is realistic about this, others even so-called friends come and visit him, and do him mischief. Listen,

Those who come to see me are not sincere; they gather bad news about me and then go out and tell it everywhere.

(verse 6) NEB

Unfortunately, human nature in its manifestly negative side is as mischievous and undermining and unfair in every age. But God's mercy and God's grace is also the same and becomes the only hope for any who fall victim to malice and misrepresentation. In practice, the cause of trouble may vary, from our own sinful action, to the injury of those who wish us ill, or seemingly inexplicable circumstances, or misfortunes that overtake us, but the effects can be the same. We become distressed in mind. Why? Yes, because we are prone to get agitated and our imagination can visualise monsters where they do not exist, and distort and poison the friendships that made us rejoice in the fellowship of other people.

Clearly the trouble involves our spiritual life. If we are sensitive to shame and sin, it is a devastating blow to lose the esteem of other people, I mean people for whom we ourselves have a high regard. We all know that such inner distress can lead to a breakdown in health and so we may get physically ill and even bedridden like the writer of this psalm. The rumour mill goes on then to interpret this as a sign of disease and predict that our days are numbered.

Sadly the fellowship of the church is sometimes not a whit behind the secular community in exhibiting this dark side of human nature. There are Christians whose track record has been one of great loyalty and faithfulness for many years, who have become victims on the tenuous basis of a mischievous letter, or a loose speculative supposition where the tongue in a swift serpent-like strike, betrays even a friend. The life of the every day world is full of this. The crowd jostling for power and position, for fame and favour, reflect a sombre analysis of basic human deficiency.

But this is not supposed to happen within the inclusive parameters of Christian ethics. It is hard to take, the psalmist makes plain, clearly commenting upon his own experience and thus relevant for others who follow the Lord and have like experiences since then. It surely was a trial of David's belief when even one who shared food at his table as Judas Iscariot did with our Lord, betrayed his trust.

> **Yea, my own familiar friend, in whom I trusted, which did eat of my bread, hath lifted up his heel against me.**
>
> (verse 9 NEB)

Suddenly he is a non-person in his church, just as surely as this happens everyday in the circles of the secular world. The hard thing for the spiritually alive person is that he has a very much increased sensitivity. Ordinary people, office - bearers as well as ministers, can be destroyed, in churches even more completely than in secular situations. Further, the church is designed to be a fellowship of tolerance of human frailty, and the purveyor of forgiveness and mercy, to cover the faults and weaknesses or sins of others. But David and sadly many others since then have found it to be quite the contrary. Thus the arrows and knives of silent condemnation and the withdrawal of fellowship of God's people, even though he has slipped up, in breach of morality or religious convention, can bring great anguish to the soul.

But stop, we are not going to dwell upon the negatives. This psalm proclaims the promise of God that those who remember the poor, whose life is one of compassion for the needy, who are therefore indwelt with the spirit of God's love, will never be forsaken by the Lord. Essentially, all the slanders and suppositions or the rumours and recycled garbage of compulsive chatterers, do not undo the fabric of grace which makes a man or a woman, a new person, the workmanship of God and chosen forever to be with him in glory. And 'if God is with us' then whatever overtakes us, even the consequences of our own sins, for no-one can escape them, we will overcome.

We can rejoice like the writer, who turned to the Lord in prayer. We are not told that we have to make an appointment for prayer to God. On the other hand, we have found that if we seek him on a regular basis in a certain place, then that time takes on a special meaning and that place, be it kneeling beside a bedside or kneeling beside the milking stool in a byre with the cows chewing the cud and munching hay in the manger, we say that place becomes hallowed with sacred memories that follow us all the days of our earthly life. But along with multitudes of disciples we have also found that when we are suddenly confronted with calamity, even before we could articulate our distress, God, our God in his mercy and his great power, has strengthened us. Such times increase our love to him and we say to you who read this, that God is never off duty, in the night nor in the day. Hear the psalmist in an other psalm as he reflects upon God's loving watchful care.

My help cometh from the Lord, which made heaven and earth.

Behold he that keeps Israel shall neither slumber nor sleep.

The Lord shall preserve thee from all evil: he shall preserve thy soul.

The Lord shall preserve thy going out and coming in from this time forth, and even for evermore.

(Psalm 121:2, 3, 7, 8)

We can understand that someone in distress turns to God in prayer. But here is evidence that he, or she and that means ourselves if we are in this trouble, can be enabled to praise God. This psalm presents us with a wonderful evidence that we can still praise God as well as bring our prayers to Him, even when we are in trouble. It surely is therapeutic advice, but also advice which has been proven in experience.

Praise the Lord, the God of Israel!

Praise him now and for ever!

Amen Amen! (verse 13 NEB)

But, Lord be merciful to me,
    and up again me raise,
That I may justly them requite
    according to thy ways.

By this I know that certainly
I favoured am by thee;
Because my hateful enemy
    triumphs not over me.

But as for me, thou me uphold'st
    in mine integrity;
And me before thy countenance
    thou sett'st continually.

The Lord, the God of Israel,
    be blessed for ever then,
From age to age eternally.
Amen, yea, and Amen.

(Scottish Psalter Psalm 41)

Psalm 102

Thou shalt arise, and have mercy upon Zion: for the time to favour her, yea, the set time, is come.

For thy saints take pleasure in her stones, and favour the dust thereof.

So the heathen shall fear the name of the Lord, and all the kings of the earth thy glory.

When the Lord shall build again Sion, he shall appear in his glory.

He will regard the prayer of the destitute, and not despise their prayer.

This shall be written for the generation to come: and the people which shall be created shall praise the Lord.

A Bird's-eye View of Life

Some time ago I had a bad attack of influenza. It lasted for a week, with the consequent indisposition which it brings. This was an epidemic. For me I could not go visiting my congregation. Also even visitation to the seven hospitals and homes for the aged was officially cancelled. On top of that when I felt recovered physically, the second sabbath arrived. But a sudden severe snow storm obliterated the landscape, blocked in the streets with huge drifts and brought cancellation of all church services.

Confined to home, I tried to occupy my time in reading and study, where I had left off. But shame on me, I had no taste for it. Looking at books increased the awful frustration I felt. What should I do? What does anyone do in similar circumstances, where they are almost violently thrown out of their busy and absorbing and satisfying routine. I can relate only what I did at the time. Having returned from a visit to Scotland some months before then I had taken notice of the traditional wheel barrow, in this case an unusually large one. The design appealed to me, as I saw it as ideal for carrying wood, which is relatively light. I had taken exact measurements of that barrow. A friend in the country had given me an old iron barrow wheel complete with axle. Though feeling very miserable and also weak, I resolved to make a wheel barrow while the 'flu' epidemic raged and the snow closed in the community. With wood salvaged from a wrecked boat, some aluminium angle from the local scrapyard, the old iron wheel, and some two dozen carriage bolts, the barrow took shape and after two weeks was completed in the manse basement. A good coat of paint inside and out, plenty grease in the bearing rests for the wheel spindle, a smoothing of the handles which were not painted, and lo! the barrow was complete and ready for use. And now, twenty years later, the barrow is as good as ever.

Do you know that all my depression disappeared. I had become so absorbed in getting the barrow made, that I had not the time to dwell on any negatives. I was so proud of my new creation, remember with old scrap wood and metal, that I suddenly felt on top of the world. With the return of normal conditions, I was completely prepared to resume my routine of private study and all my pastoral and preaching duties with a new zest and energy. How true the saying, *A change of activity is often as good as a rest.* That is a very real justification for us all to have some physical recreation, to prevent us from becoming spiritual neurotics.

We cannot always make a wheel barrow when we are under the weather, or having a bad day. It is also true that if we love God and become as it were dependent upon him, then any break in that communion, any absence of that fellowship grieves the heart.

In the New English Bible translation the title of this psalm is given as 'The prayer of a troubled young man.' But one would have to add, 'who knows the Lord.' It must be conceded that the believer is like anyone else, vulnerable to the awful visitations of depression and disturbed peace, common to human experience. This valley is a graphic picture which David paints of his condition. We should indeed ask as we look at the psalm, How does it fit into the didactic pattern of the church? What does this say to us? Is it good or bad? Is it normal or abnormal? Is it healthy or unhealthy? Are we justified in saying that here is an ideal or an example that we should emulate? Listen to this.

**My days are consumed like smoke, and my
bones are burned as the hearth.**

My heart is smitten, and withered like grass.

**By reason of the voice of my groanings, my
bones cleave to my skin.**

**I am like a bittern. I am like an owl. (I am
like a lonely wee bird) NEB**

**My life is disappearing like smoke; my body
is burning like fire.**

It is very likely that this trouble so vividly expressed, is
linked with his physical condition. The graphic description
given by the question is, Did his spiritual troubles bring on this
grim physical condition.? The Psalmist, indicates that
physically, he is in a very bad way. The condition? Or was he
so sick with some fever and with this his whole system became
run down?

The loneliness of trouble

David sees himself like a sparrow alone sitting on top of
the house, looking down on all the human activity. It is a
situation which grieves him for by nature he likes human
company and to be an integral part of everyday life. He feels
estranged from people, who he sees as vindictive, and as having
sworn against him. He is insulted and reproached continually
by his enemies. That is a sad state to be in. For David like you
and me was not a loner, and to feel that he was ostracised,
even to imagine this, meant that he was deprived of the joy
and happiness of fellowship of friends and neighbours, his peers
in work, and the feeling of belonging to the community at large.

He makes clear that he felt spiritual alienation, as if God
also had withdrawn his favour.

**For I have eaten ashes like bread, and
mingled my drink with weeping.**

And he adds,

> **Because of thine indignation and thy wrath:**
> **for thou hast lifted me up, and cast me down.**

If it is his spiritual condition which brought this grim situation about, then this Psalm has a lesson for every believer which is quite clear. Our religion, even as Christians should never get us into this mess. Christ came to give peace of mind and heart and spirit along with health and wholeness. There is something wrong with a religion or a variation of religion, if when applied to ourselves, the truth of God and his great love to us, brings us this kind of awful mental and physical symptoms of distress.

Trouble of the kind suggested here can often be linked with physical illness. Some suggest that David wrote this when he was a young man. If so he was used to being out both day and night. The perception of David as king living in the comfort of his palace is incomplete. Before his ascendancy to the throne as king and after it, he spent many months each year as military commander in various wars. This put great stress on one's physical health in the sharply contrasting temperatures of Palestine. When we think how vulnerable people are at the end of the 20th century, with all the benefits of warm anoraks and medicinal aids to counteract the common cold, the flu and other fevers, how much more was David in his contemporary world! He could have contracted some form of malaria, living out in the contrasting temperatures of night and day, summer and winter.

The psalm could have been written when he was much older, and yet subject to bouts of his physical trouble. In the two world wars earlier in the 20th century, many young soldiers contracted disease, both in the European war theatres and in the Far East, especially in the Burma campaign. Some died, others came back to civilian life yet every so often suffered from recurring bouts of illnesses like malaria.

This Psalm is not a progression like many other psalms, from depression to optimism, from despair to hope. There is no message here where we examine a perceived spiritual problem, and then see the remedial process, whereby the person ends up fully recovered by appropriating God's remedy. There is indeed a problem here, that is very obvious. This person graphically describes a grim human condition, of personal, mental and physical trouble. Many of us can identify ourselves with this and our own visitations of trouble now or at some time in our experience. But let us not automatically blame this awful experience on our faith. If indeed our faith produces something like this, then there is something wrong with our faith.

But as we suggested, why exclude the very obvious possibility that this trouble - depression was surely in part due to a physical cause! Was David not undermined by some fever and still a long way from 'getting on his feet' as it were?

The fact that he composes a psalm at this time and includes a description of his own spiritual and physical condition is not evidence that this is to be interpreted as having a spiritual cause.

We have a comparable description in the Book of Job. He answers Bildad's accusation of presumption. In the description of his trouble, he says. *My bone cleaveth to my skin.* (Job 19: 20). David also says here in verse 5, My bones cleave unto my skin.

Dr Robert Young points out in his great Analytical Concordance, that Job, whether as a historical or metaphorical figure is introduced to believers to teach two things, namely *that true religion is not based on selfish considerations* and secondly, *that temporal calamities are not always the consequences of sin.*

The specific disease with which Job was smitten is not disclosed to us. But the effects are there, a comprehensive list of all the possible calamities which can overtake a person. Yet as Dr Young points out, it is not a spiritual condition of going astray, or sinning which we all know brings trouble, which has caused this physiological effect where the whole person is troubled. Rather the condition is traced to one or more physical cause. Then, as troubles do not come alone, one evil effect leads to another and soon we have a catalogue of calamities.

There is no doubt that when we believe that God loves us, that he rules over our life in Providence as well as in the redemptive grace of the Gospel, this does not mean that we are exempted from all the sufferings of this life which are the lot of other people. We can call this God's Permissive Will.

Some years ago, a Scot, Dougal Robertson, had his wooden sailboat sink under him, in an encounter with a whale near the Galapagos Islands. During the months when the family - three adults and two children - balanced themselves in an eight foot long dinghy in the middle of the Pacific Ocean, no storm came to swamp them, no sharks came to puncture the rubber raft that they used to carry the little gear they had salvaged. He, an agnostic, relates how his wife prayed every day and witnessed to her faith in the power of God and the conviction that he was watching over them to bless them. And it seems to come through in the narrative of the crusty Scot that something of his wife's faith was having an effect upon himself, although at the time he was not willing to admit it openly. I believe that the Dougal Robertson who came through that experience of saving providence, must have become a very different person. The fact is that time and again, trouble is blessed to us.

It is good to hear that a wife can be used as a blessing to husband and home. *A virtuous woman is a crown to her husband.* (Proverbs12:4) We, by nature will not listen to wisdom, because of our pride and prejudice; often men will not listen to the advice of women and especially their wives. By nature man thinks he know better than women. But women are by nature more susceptible to the spiritual. This is reasonable, since they come close to death in the experience of childbirth, without which human life itself would die within four generations.

Meeting adversity makes us think about basic truths

Adversity or trouble is a shake -up of our complacency and smug self-righteousness. Trouble disturbs the very atoms in the molecular structure of our spiritual nature. In other words, it makes us think. It is as if we are like the iron that is made white hot by the smith, in the furnace, for it is only then that he can beat it into a particular shape, a horse shoe or an anchor. David knew this deep down. He writes in Psalm 119, verse 71.

> *It is good for me to be afflicted; that I might*
> *learn thy statutes.*

We do know that all kinds of troubles can be blessed to us. We do not see this at the time but afterwards, when we can look back and see that our loving heavenly Father did not forsake us, and would never cause us to suffer beyond our endurance. The fact is that God teaches us by troubles, so that we are humbled, and come to realise that we are dependent upon him. And in learning this we get to know our Lord more and more as we call upon him for his needed help. Just think of it like going to your favourite shop for groceries. You get to know the person who serves. Christ our Lord is known to us through the Spirit who serves us at the Throne of Grace and Supplication. Nothing will satisfy the hungry soul except the things of Christ, even those that are stamped with the Cross, for this is the hallmark of Divine Love, and the Bread that cometh down from above, that nourishes the soul. And though we do not see our Lord in a sensory way, when we are spiritually minded, we see Him in all his loveliness and all his sufficiency. Just as we will buy only the branded good that we have come to trust and for which we have developed a taste, so believers once they have set their hearts on the spiritual provisions of the Cross, will not be content with anything less.

Reconciling suffering with love

No-one has been able to reconcile suffering with love. They seem, humanly speaking irreconcilable, contradictory, incompatible. That is if we see them as separate. But they are not really separate. They are both aspects of human life and human life is not abstract but is represented in the unity of each person. Love does not exist in one person, and suffering in the life of another. Both are found in the experience of one person and therefore must be perceived as inextricably involved with each other. In the devotional experience of a living faith, we see an answer in that love has the capacity and willingness to suffer. Read St Paul's definition of love, *Charity suffereth long.* (Ist Corinthians 13:4)

Apart from understanding the inseparableness of love and suffering, God's will for us is not to augment the love we have as human beings. He gives us to love in a different way, a way that is inextricably linked to our own reception of the God's free gift of love. His will for us is to discover the *new commandment.* (John 13: 34). To know the love of God, and in turn to love as God wants us to do, and to show us the way of love in Christ, is the goal of revelation.

Thus there is no contradiction if we think of God's over-all will for us, when we encounter suffering or adversity. The contradiction exists when we seek to resolve the question of suffering, without the governing principle of God's will for us, which is to love as he in Christ has showed us.

Some would suggest that here in the psalm before us, we see the symptoms of a nervous breakdown. But then many people hit rock bottom in a temporary depression linked with the visitation of a fever. The remarkable point illustrated here is that David had this condition of affliction, but that he was rational and articulate and able to record it, in the context of a living faith, a faith that not only embraces prayer to God in distress, but also meditation on his law and singing praises him for his mercy. Here is encouragement for all of us , that we in turn in succeeding generations, might be strengthened and reassured that we can overcome, and *be more than conquerors through him that loved us*. It says a lot for David - remember, he had no tape recorder.

Think again of Job in his affliction. We clearly see that a physical cause can affect the whole person, and bring on further physical troubles as well as spiritual distress. On the other hand we do know the opposite, that a physiological cause can bring on physical symptoms of suffering. But this latter is no ideal to entertain in our minds, or accept as inevitable. It is no norm of belief to accept as good. Obviously it is only good, when we are buoyant in faith and full of joy and hope and confidence. Then there is the corollary that we expect, of feeling physically good.

But here we are looking at the negative. When we think of Jesus, our Saviour, in his sufferings in the Garden of Gethsemane, he said,

> *My soul is exceedingly sorrowful, even unto death.*

> (Matthew 26:38)

And Luke records the physical effects of this spiritual sorrow which filled the heart of the Saviour as he bore the sins of the world in his own body, to make atonement

> *And being in an agony he prayed more earnestly and his sweat was as it were great drops of blood falling to the ground.*

Christ's Sufferings are unique

Jesus does not portray here an example for us to follow. Such perception of his suffering leads to false efforts of emulation, which in turn deflect our minds from understanding the vicarious nature of the Cross, and the singular and unrepeatable act it represents of Divine redemptive love. Though it was in the will of God, it was God's decretive will that he should suffer, and in the context of human society which he came to redeem.

Further what he endured was the effects of sin, when he bore our sins in his own body on the Cross. So that both in his actual crucifixion, at the hands of Church and State, and in the anticipation of it, the suffering was the effect of evil, endemic in unregenerate human nature and expressed in the rejection of the Christ as the Son of God. There is no reason to believe that if Christ should appear in our period of history, that his advent would meet with anything less than that which followed in the sequence of events that met the King of kings and the Prince of Peace, as recorded in the Gospels.

After his Resurrection did not Jesus meet the disciples to enlighten them so that they understood the Scriptures which he had come to fulfill.

> *And he said unto them, These are the words which I spake unto you, while I was yet with you, that all things must be fulfilled which were written in the law of Moses, and in the **prophets** and in the **psalms** concerning me. Then opened he their understanding, that they might understand the scriptures. And said unto them, Thus it is written and thus it behoved Christ to suffer, and to rise from the day on the third day: And that repentance and remission of sins should be preached in his name among all nations, beginning at Jerusalem.*

(St Luke 24:44 - 47)

Notice Jesus refers to himself as being the subject of psalms, though not by name. Thus we have Psalms like Psalm 22, (verse 14, 17,18) where we see a picture of anguish and also of prophecy with regard to the clothes that our Saviour wore, when he was arrested by the soldiers.

> *I am poured out like water, and all my bones are out of joint: my heart is like wax. I may tell all my bones: they look and stare at me. They parted my garments among them.*

But we must guard against thinking that just because Jesus suffered in this respect in his role of Redeemer, that Christians should look for guilt every time suffering overtakes them. Jesus was heavy at heart, bearing the sin of the world. We are set free, for *burdens are lifted at Calvary,* as the hymn says. His heart was so heavy that in physical terms, it is thought that he died literally of a broken heart. What a thought, hear that, the Son of God who came from glory, died of a broken heart for you and me. How can we ever forget this, the love that did this. But our sins required a love like this, that would suffer until the heart burst, so that the Saviour died. But He has set us free. For Jesus' heart broke, not just figuratively, but physically, because his heart spiritually was so heavy, bearing the burden of the sins of humanity, alone. (Luke 22:44)

A reason for continual rejoicing

This means that we are to rejoice. Christ has won, and given us the victory. We are to rejoice like the apostles who returned to Jerusalem worshipping God, with great joy. And the apostle Paul tells us also to rejoice.

> *Rejoice in the Lord alway: and again I say, Rejoice.*

> (Philippians 4:4)

We have then two opposite poles as the cause of suffering. On the one hand the **physical** exemplified in the character of Job. On the other hand the **spiritual** represented by Jesus the Christ. How strange that the Son of God should be quoted as a sinner. But it had to be, he had to become a sin-bearer, because our sins were imputed to him, that his righteousness might be imputed to us in a Covenant of Grace whereby we receive the Atonement.

> *For he hath made him to be (a sin offering)*
> *for us who knew no sin, that we might be made*
> *the righteousness of God in him.*

(2 Corinthians 5:21)

Grieving for loved ones

There is another situation which can bring anguish and suffering. The suffering may come to us because of the view we take of outward circumstances. One of the effects of living in Christ, is that we yearn for loved ones above all else that they find the joy of salvation.

When we see them going the wrong way, often following their own will under the influence of peer pressure and the prevailing climate of the world, which is hostile to Christ, our hearts grieve and the normal interests of life are turned to ashes for us. Is this not the picture we have illustrated in the life of David in relation to his son Absalom especially? But the great thing is that though he was at a low ebb, like a boat when the tide is low which still is afloat, so David's faith was still buoyant. His faith was still alive. However low we may feel, however much we may feel that we are close to rock-bottom, for whatever reason, yet our faith can still be strong. You know, it does not matter whether there is only a foot of water under the keel of a boat or a thousand feet, the boat will float. And that is what counts, whether it is a little rowboat, or a massive cargo ship. Remember that, let us never give up our faith.

In fact this is often the very test of our faith. We are not to judge faith by its performance on the mountain top. We are not to gauge faith by the fervour of the soul in the warm fellowship of the prayer meeting - we have a wistful longing for such experiences. We all know that we love these and the great gatherings of believers in worship. In these, we are uplifted so that we could say with the apostle Paul that we understand how a soul may feel lifted up into heavenly places. This personal experience is not just subjective but becomes the experience of the congregation where God is in the midst with the grace and the glory that alone are his. And God in the presence of the Holy Spirit never comes without the abundance of his grace and the multitude of his mercies. That is why those who come and worship him with hearts that have been emptied of all other desires are filled with a sense of his glory and his grace. But we have to look at a person when faith is tried, when he is *down*. That is when we are tested. Notice there is nothing wrong with the faith. It is just that circumstances are like the tide, so that the water is at a low ebb.

Circumstances at a low ebb

David said, speaking to God, of his permissive will.
Thou hast lifted me up, and cast me down.

verse 10

(You picked me up, And threw me away.)

NEB

The remarkable thing is that David's faith was still alive. But that is the wonderful message for us here in this Psalm. Here is a song for the sanctuary and here is a song for the heart, a song of praise to God. It is true that the psalm reveals the introspective searching of the believer's own heart. But after all we are human, however strong our faith may be. And is it not true that many people who do not live by faith in Christ and the efficacy of his redeeming work, often have second

97

thoughts and are often uneasy within themselves? Suddenly as it came to king Belshazzar of old, right in the middle of the party, the handwriting of God appears with the indictment, **Thou art found wanting.**

But David is turning to God with his groans. He does not go to a psychiatrist. He does not moan to his friends and make life intolerable for others. They have their own troubles as we all well know. David gives us the lead. He takes his troubles to God. That is faith. For God never turns away the needy. It his great work to use all the glorious expedients in Christ to minister to us so that we get through the toughest times and experiences and at last make it to our eternal home. Thus we have a wonderful example illustrated for us here.

David's prayer has the evidence of a positive faith

This faith is not dormant. It is not asleep. It is not switched to automatic. It is on manual control, requiring first person studied action. It is still active. Some might say that David's faith was dead. But if you took the spiritual pulse, it would still be there, albeit not as strong as it might be. But faith when it is alive at all confirms, namely, that David and all the children of faith **will never die.** Notice these observations for they are given for our strengthening and encouragement when we are afflicted.

A live faith means that God will hear us.

Listen to David, linking his own condition to all believers past, present and yet to be born.

> **He will regard the prayer of the destitute,**
> **And not despise their prayer.**

> **verse** 17

Do you see what this means? It does not mean that every time we suffer, we must have faith to believe that we will be exempt from that experience because we are privileged as God's people. Rather God will give us grace to bear it. Further, our faith may well be smitten. It may get muddied when we have fallen. But that is not the end of it. It still has a pulse, a heart-beat. Our strength comes from the power of the Lord who is with us as the friend *that sticketh closer than a brother.* Knowing that a friend is with us on a dark night is a great comfort. And knowing that when we fall or get into trouble, that the friend will not run away and forsake us is a glorious comfort. And that is what God offers in the terms of discipleship. He will never let us down. He is a very *present help in time of trouble.* (Psalm 46:1) And our Lord told the disciples, *Lo I am with you always.* (Matthew 28:20)

Also there is this, David believed that God was now ready and present to pour out blessings on his church. He believed that the time set by God himself in his sovereign will had come and now was, for God to show his lovingkindnesses and his glorious mercy. What a thought, God's mercy? Did you hear that? The time has come for mercy from heaven to be poured out upon his church. And therefore anyone in it at that time whose heart is open, can be blessed. Think what this means for those who long for mercy. Think of those assailed by doubt; those who are tempted to think that they are not covered by the spiritual terms of the Covenant, because their faith is so tenuous. Listen, mercy flows from heaven; grace in all the efficacy of the Cross comes to the lowly, the contrite, those who have left their own righteousness outside and come into his presence with God's people, so that they have the righteousness of Christ. The heart believes. Who can spell out the emotions of the heart that is open to the Spirit of God, the heart of the person whose soul, pant*s like a deer for the living waters. (*Psalm 40:1)

A living faith reaches beyond oneself.

Hear the affirmation of faith as it reaches out in a comprehensive concern for the church.

**For thy servants take pleasure in her stones,
and favour the dust thereof.**

**When the Lord shall again build up Zion,
he shall appear in his glory**

verse 14, 16

You see, the goal of our faith is not egocentric. We are called effectually by God's grace to forget about ourselves, and be Christ-centred, and church -conscious. When we are so disposed, we take the burdens of the world, and bring them to Christ and bring Christ to them. For it is from the rock quarry of a broken humanity, that the stones are cut and hewed, and shaped and prepared, for the building of Zion the house of God and the city of God. Was this not prefigured in the building of the house of God by Solomon!

And the house, when it was in building, was built of stone made ready before it was brought thither: so that there was neither hammer nor axe nor any tool of iron heard in the house, while it was in building.

(Ist Kings 6:7)

While there is personal salvation through Christ, and every soul, yet the glory of God, in the redemptive metamorphosis of humanity on a world scale is designed to bring about a transformed world. This means a new era, an eternal one of humanity. That is a primary aim of our faith. You see the glory we think of personally, must be the glory of God and this is made manifest in his church.

**So the heathen shall fear the name of the
Lord, and all the kings of the earth thy glory**

(verse 15)

Thus a believer who has an unquestioning faith that he is saved, and yet does not believe in the positive purpose of God being fulfilled in a redeemed society, leaves a real difficulty to be resolved.

Trouble's Perspective

David describes how he feels, namely his own desolation. Sometimes we feel desolate and see this as being *lost in the crowd*. David here portrays his desolation as one who is abstracted from the crowd. He sees himself apart from all the warmth and fellowship which is surely the accompaniment of faith in the interaction of service and worship wherever our lot is cast in the Providence of God. He says he is like a little sparrow, forlorn and desolate, sitting on top of a house. In another psalm he speaks of the sparrow, building a nest under the eaves of the house of God .

> *With my whole being I sing for joy to the living God*
>
> *Even the sparrows have built a nest and the swallows have their own home*
>
> (Psalm 84:2 - 3)

On the other hand when he is afflicted, he adds that he is also like the lonely bittern or the desert owl. All these birds are not just alone. **They are acute observers.** They are apart from the crowd. Their loneliness gives them a certain perspective. They look on the world going along in all its numerous activities, and they observe. They do not feel that they are p*art of the show.* But then let us go back to the wee sparrow. I think David must have been fond of sparrows. He says,

> **I watch and am as a sparrow alone upon the housetop.**

But his faith operates. He still sees as it were with the eye of faith, and though his heart is heavy and his whole condition at an alltime **low,** David articulates his perception. We have taken note of his self-perception or the way he spelt out his own condition, albeit in the context of the church. But we are bound to take note also of the observations he makes here, outwith himself. You see, he is not on the mountain. Then it would be reasonable for him to speak of God's glory and the land that is afar off. All believers have this experience at one time or another in their pilgrimage. They are sustained in dark days by such thoughts that come back to them to encourage them to keep going.

But what is precious here is to look at an **afflicted soul** looking outward from himself and his desolation and taking note of his observations.

The Bird's-eye View

Three definite observations are made which are valid for the afflicted. God endures forever; God always hears sincere prayer; no affliction, however hard can destroy our faith.

What an assurance for us all in a changing world, that provides no certainty even in the astro-physical context, where our little planet is like a speck of dust in the myriad galaxies of 'stars' that fill the universe!

Thy years are throughout all generations
verse 24

What a thought! God endures forever. David believes that all generations will remember God. He sees prophetically as he looks, from the vantage point of the sparrow on the housetop, and as he looks down the road of history, he believes that people in every age will remember God through all the eons of existence. Hear his confidence in another psalm,

> *And everyone will praise you for all time to come. My soul will keep your fame alive forever,*

(Psalm 45:17) NEB

It is not as if you have to feel desolation like a lonely sparrow on a housetop or a desert owl alone in the wilderness, to have this view. We should have this perspective of faith all the time, and surely when things are going well and when we are full of optimism and hope. The great thing here is that **no affliction can destroy faith.** We can feed on God's glory as well as upon God's grace. Thus we see a parallel expressed in that immortal doxology, thought to be added by David's son Solomon at the end of Psalm 72 which we in the Christian church identify with God's Son Jesus the Christ.

> *His name shall endure forever: his name shall*
> *be continued as long as the sun: and men shall*
> *be blessed in him: all nations shall call him*
> *blessed.*
>
> *Blessed be the Lord God, the God of Israel,*
> *who only doeth wondrous things.*
>
> *And blessed be his glorious name forever: and*
> *let the whole earth be filled with his glory;*
> *Amen and Amen*

(Psalm 72:17 - 19)

This liturgy of prayer and praise, has priority before all other compositions, however glorious and beautiful these may be. For many like-minded believers there is a quiet belief that in the absence of any other, the psalms will be the immortal manual of praise, in the celestial city of the redeemed. No, there is no future except as a local relative term for each generation here in this life. Heaven is already full of glory with multitudes who worship the Lamb who washed them and saved them from all their sins and made them kings and priests unto God, to live in the realms of the heavenly within the veil. By faith we are already part of this, sealed in the immutable Covenant of Grace by the Blood of Christ.

When our physical life ends, the curtain of the flesh is drawn aside and the soul that loved the Lord is taken into the heavenly. All the senses of hearing, of seeing of feeling are given a new and spiritual capacity to behold the glory of the Saviour. Thus we speak of the eternal here in the present when the Lord is with us in his spirit.

But we also think of it in another way. We look to heaven, as coming at last into the presence of the eternal. Christians have all, as heirs of God and joint heirs with Christ. It is just that when the great change comes from the physical to the metaphysical, our consciousness is no longer restricted by our worldly environment, nor limited to the sensory. We come into the eternal. We are set free. Our souls embrace the greatness of glory. We become absorbed with all the wonders of heaven. It is all beyond what we can think of here. But it is all true and all ours, through Christ Jesus our Lord.

> *For the promises of God in him are yea, and*
> *in him Amen, unto the glory of God by us*
> (1st Corinthians 1: 2

Thou shalt arise and mercy yet
Thou to mount Sion shalt extend:
Her time for favour which was set,
Behold is now come to an end.

Thy saints take pleasure in her stones,
Her very dust to them is dear.
All heathen lands and kingly thrones
On earth thy glorious name shall fear.

God in his glory shall appear,
When Sion he builds and repairs,
He shall regard and lend his ear
Unto the needy's humble prayer.

(Scottish Psalter 2nd Version Psalm 102)